RITUAL AND RECORD

Recent Titles in
Contributions to the Study of World History

The Practical Revolutionaries: A New Interpretation of the French Anarchosyndicalists
Barbara Mitchell

The Dragon and the Wild Goose: China and India
Jan Taylor

Land and Freedom: The Origins of Russian Terrorism, 1876–1879
Deborah Hardy

Young Guard! The Communist Youth League, Petrograd 1917–1920
Isabel A. Tirado

Engine of Mischief: An Analytical Biography of Karl Radek
Jim Tuck

Central America: Historical Perspectives on the Contemporary Crises
Ralph Lee Woodward, Jr., editor

The Free Germany Movement: A Case of Patriotism or Treason?
Kai P. Schoenhals

Victims and Survivors: Displaced Persons and Other War Victims in Viet-Nam, 1954
Louis A. Wiesner

Tsar Paul and the Question of Madness: An Essay in History and Psychology
Hugh Ragsdale

The Orphan Stone: The Minnesinger Dream of Reich
Richard J. Berleth

American Constitutionalism Abroad: Selected Essays in Comparative
Constitutional History
George Athan Billias, editor

Appeasement in Europe: A Reassessment of U.S. Policies
David F. Schmitz and Richard D. Challener, editors

RITUAL AND

RECORD

Sports Records and Quantification in Pre-Modern Societies

Edited by **John Marshall Carter**
and **Arnd Krüger**

Contributions to the Study of World History, Number 17

GREENWOOD PRESS

New York • Westport, Connecticut • London

Library of Congress Cataloging-in-Publication Data

Ritual and record : sports records and quantification in pre-modern
  societies / edited by John Marshall Carter and Arnd Krüger.
    p.   cm.—(Contributions to the study of world history, ISSN
  0885–9159 ; no. 17)
    Includes bibliographical references.
    ISBN 0–313–25699–3 (lib. bdg. : alk. paper)
    1. Guttmann, Allen. From ritual to record.   2. Sports—Social
aspects.   3. Sports—Social aspects—United States.   4. Sports—
Records—History.   I. Carter, John Marshall.   II. Krüger, Arnd.
III. Series.
GV706.5.R59   1990
306.4′83–dc20   89–78452

British Library Cataloguing in Publication Data is available.

Library of Congress Catalog Card Number: 89–78452
ISBN: 0–313–25699–3
ISSN: 0885–9159

First published in 1990

Greenwood Press, Inc.
88 Post Road West, Westport, Connecticut 06881

Printed in the United States of America

The paper used in this book complies with the
Permanent Paper Standard issued by the National
Information Standards Organization (Z39.48–1984).

10 9 8 7 6 5 4 3 2 1

Contents

Preface

The contributors to the present volume discovered each other, as is often the case with scholars separated by oceans and different languages, because of their response to Allen Guttmann's *From Ritual to Record: The Nature of Modern Sports* (1978). In the developing field of sports history, Professor Guttmann's book was widely praised, especially by scholars in this new field. In the present volume, Guttmann's thesis about sports records is examined by a wider variety of scholars from Europe, the United States, Canada, and Japan.

This work has developed rather slowly over the past four years. In 1985 I was fortunate enough to be able to visit the Federal Republic of Germany to do research on my own specialty, sports in the Middle Ages. I was still more fortunate to be hosted by Professor Arnd Krüger of the Institut für Sportwissenschaften at the University of Göttingen. Professor Krüger and I immediately discovered that in our response to Professor Guttmann's *From Ritual to Record*, we were on a similar wavelength. If the idea for the present volume did not arise during my stay in West Germany, then it surely evolved through our correspondence over the years that followed.

The present volume has been a very difficult undertaking for several reasons. For one thing, the German, Danish, and Japanese contributors have been asked to write their chapters in English. Their painstaking efforts should be applauded. Another problem has been the nagging process of mailing chapters around the world. Nevertheless, through it all, the book has developed, and it is hoped that readers will find it a useful contribution to the field of sports history.

In the introduction, the editors attempt to place the thesis advanced by Guttmann in *From Ritual to Record* within a broad social and historical context, as well as within a proper historiographical context. Donald Parkerson's "The New Sport History" looks at the Guttmann thesis within the context of the new social history.

The next seven chapters fall into the chronological progression of historical sports development within Western civilization, although two of the chapters contain information about areas outside the boundaries of Western civilization—Japan and the Hawaiian Islands before the coming of the English. Wolfgang Decker's chapter, "The Record of the Ritual: The Athletic Records of Ancient Egypt," investigates the possibility of sports records in Egypt during the New Kingdom. Dietrich Ramba then chronicles what he terms "Recordmania in Sports in Ancient Greece and Rome." John Marshall Carter looks for sports records in the explosion of literacy, bureaucracy, and chivalry in England in the twelfth and thirteenth centuries. John McClelland analyzes Renaissance sports manuals and what they divulge in his "The Numbers of Reason: Luck, Logic, and Art in Renaissance Conceptions of Sport." Joachim Rühl then analyzes tournament scoring cheques in "Sports Quantification in Tudor and Elizabethan Tournaments." Gundolf Krüger explores the possibility of sports records in a non-Western setting in his "Sport in the Context of Non-European Cultural Tradition: The Example of Hawaii." Arnd Krüger and Akira Ito weigh the validity of the Guttmann thesis in "On the Limitations of Eichberg's and Mandell's Theory of Sports and Their Quantification in View of *Chikaraishi*."

The next three chapters do not fit as well into the traditional chronological scheme. Although each includes material relevant to Western sports records, the approach of the chapters that follow by Ove Korsgaard, Henning Eichberg, and Arnd Krüger differs from that of the preceding chapters. Korsgaard's "Sport As a Practice of Religion: The Record As Ritual" emphasizes the religious aspects of sports. Eichberg looks at the development of records in his "Stronger, Funnier, Deadlier: Track and Field on the Way to the Ritual of the Record." And Krüger employs sociobiological methodology in his chapter entitled "The Ritual in Modern Sport: A Sociobiological Approach."

In the final chapter, Allen Guttmann responds to the contributors and reexamines his own original view in light of more recent investigations. His chapter "Rituals, Records, Responses" closes what the editors and contributors hope is a useful attempt to widen the debate over the origins of sports records.

The editors would like to thank the contributors for their hard work and Cynthia Harris of Greenwood Press for her interest in and sensitivity to this project. The editors and contributors would like to thank Maureen Melino and Meg Fergusson of Greenwood Press for their help in bringing the book to fruition. And finally, the editors would also like to thank the Deutscher Akademischer Austauschdienst for their support of John Marshall Carter's research in West Germany, which led ultimately to the creation of this project.

—John Marshall Carter

RITUAL AND RECORD

Introduction

JOHN MARSHALL CARTER AND ARND KRÜGER

The scholarly discussion of sport and quantification, ritual and record, goes back fifteen years and over the past nine years has evolved into somewhat of a controversy. It has occupied some of the most productive minds in the field. In 1974, when Henning Eichberg published his "Auf Zoll und Quintlein. Sport und Quantifizierungsprozess in der frühen Neuzeit," he showed that modern quantification techniques began in the Italian Renaissance, but that modern sports, with their measuring and recording of *citius-altius-fortius* (faster-higher-stronger), started much later.[1] Eichberg's own studies were centered in Germany[2] and Sumatra[3] during the eighteenth century and his main emphasis was on shifts in the public discourse. He found that in Germany rational philanthropists replaced refined, geometric, rococo exercises with attempts to quantify the results of children,[4] whereas in the non-European culture nonmeasuring and noncompetitive sport had been dominant.[5]

The concept of the relatively late invention of the sports record was further developed by Richard D. Mandell who described it with the simple formula: "The idea of a record is young."[6] In his original presentation[7] he tried to theorize further by using Walter Rostow's economic theory of takeoff into sustained growth[8] to find a common denominator that could explain why the keeping of records was taking place in different countries at different times. Using Maria Kloeren's *Sport und Rekord*[9] together with Eichberg's earlier works,[10] Mandell placed the beginning of modern sports records in the Industrial Revolution. He also noted that some other modern features like democracy and rationalization, which were common parts of modern sports, distinguished sports records from earlier versions. He noted that "in fact the sports record was invented very late.

The first use of 'record' [in connection with a sports performance] that I have found appeared in a training manual for track and field athletes published in 1868 and lists 'the best performances on record.' ''[11]

This important paper led in two directions, one affirmative and another contradictory. Allen Guttmann was encouraged to complete the theory in his *From Ritual to Record*,[12] where he claimed that modern sports are characterized by

• Secularism.
• Equality of opportunity to compete and in the conditions of competition.
• Specialization of roles.
• Rationalization
• Bureaucratic organization.
• Quantification.
• The quest for records.[13]

These characteristics are to a remarkable degree those of modern society as described by Max Weber and Talcott Parsons.[14] Guttmann took up the question of quantification by stating:

The mathematical discoveries of the seventeenth century were popularized in the eighteenth century, at which time we can observe the beginnings of our modern obsession with quantification in sport. During the Age of Enlightenment, we can see the transition from the Renaissance concept of "measure," in the sense of moderation and balance, to the modern concept of measurement. The movement is philologically visible in German as well, i.e., from *Mass* to *Messen*.[15]

On the other hand, on the occasion of the International Seminar of Physical Education and Sports History in Tokyo Arnd Krüger noted that there was an original line of recordkeeping in Japan[16] which had nothing to do with Western civilization or the Industrial Revolution. Records of the performances of the *Chikaraishi* (weightlifters) rice carriers were used to demonstrate their superiority and became the basis for rational comparison over time and space. The quantity of rice bags lifted was the basis of comparison, the priests guaranteed the measurement, and the record lists were kept in the temple shrines. When the joint German-Japanese paper by Arnd Krüger and Akira Ito was published in 1979,[17] Mandell and Eichberg contradicted the findings.[18] In this Eichberg showed that his position was quite different from Mandell's: "I have never maintained that modern performance quantification spread from Britain; on the contrary, I have shown that corresponding tendencies developed independently on the European continent among the philanthropists of the eighteenth century and the early gymnasts."[19]

In the postscript to the second edition of *Der Weg des Sports in die industrielle Zivilisation*[20] Eichberg took up the discussion in a broader sense and agreed that Krüger and Ito had rightfully questioned the link between sports and the process of rationalization as a particular European development. He vehemently contradicted the other concept of the paper, that certain human features are universal and "natural" and that under certain conditions they can therefore be found everywhere.[21]

The question of when modern thinking in athletics began was taken up a year later when the UCLA Center for Medieval and Renaissance Studies held the international seminar on the athlete and the emergence of modern spirit.[22] Some of the papers read at that meeting were later published in German translation under the provocative title *Die Anfänge des modernen Sports in der Renaissance* [The Beginning of Modern Sports in the Renaissance]. This work showed that the rationalization which characterized the Renaissance man was also prominent in sports. The shift which Eichberg and Guttmann claimed took place in the Baroque era was anticipated by other shifts. Eichberg, looking at sports in the eighteenth and nineteenth centuries instead of earlier periods, did not realize that geometrical forms were yet another form of quantification.[23] McClelland showed for the example of acrobatics that records were attempted and generally propagated as extraordinary performances. The laws of biomechanics were introduced in the practice of highly paid professionals.[24] Modern rational thinking became part of training theory in the Renaissance and remained valid into the twentieth century. For the example of swimming, Krüger showed that the shift from learning by imitation to learning by following the laws of nature, from fear of the elements to experiments with the elements, from nature as threat to nature as tool, marked the beginning of all modern physical education and sports.[25]

Krüger's position was, of course, contradicted by Guttmann in his review of the book. In this review Guttmann made the fine differentiation that it was important to know whether the quantification was done as an expression of rationalization or for the explicit use of setting records. In the latter sense, a record is a precisely measured performance which is universally accepted and which surpasses all previously achieved performances.[26] In this sense he acknowledged that Tuccaro did break a record by jumping through ten hoops instead of the previous eight in a *salto mortale*. The authority to validate the performance was the king at whose court Tuccaro performed his great feat.[27]

The Krüger/Ito argument was supported by William Baker who claimed that humankind has a natural tendency to exhibit, to perform, to show off, to illustrate physical superiority.

Human beings cannot live by bread alone. They dream and they strive. Not merely for warmth do they take fire from the altars of the gods; curiosity is their glory and their pain. They climb mountains, cross uncharted seas, and explore outer space for reasons other than material benefits. They thrive on challenges. Seekers of laurels, they especially measure themselves in competition with fellow humans. Where there is no contest, they create one. From deep within, and from millennia past, comes the impulse for athletic competition.[28]

But is there also an impulse to record the sports performance and and to compete against such a record, to be better than the best man or woman "on record"?

As could have been expected, in his world history of sport Mandell came to quite a different conclusion. In his *Sport: A Cultural History*, he accepts "something we might call 'nascent sports records' "[29] in pre-Meji Japan, but his emphasis is on "England: Land of Sport." He altogether omits the complexity of Italian Renaissance sports on the continent and shows little awareness of the folk traditions of sports and games in Europe. It is obvious that it is impossible to write a world history of sports, cultural or otherwise, and not leave something out, but Mandell overstresses his point that "sport as we know it [was] more or less . . . invented by Englishmen." He also contends that "in Central and Eastern Europe . . . recreational activities—designed as physical education, popular gymnastics, paramilitary training, or the preparation of national teams— have long been a matter of informed debate and, subsequently, purposeful direction."[30]

The construction of such a sharp dichotomy is unrealistic, for it leaves out the research on British sport education by James A. Mangan and others,[31] as well as much of the work on continental sports from tournaments to folk games by Roland Renson and many others.[32] As his reviewer, Stephen Hardy, notes, Mandell "slights the constitutive nature of pre-modern sport. Indeed, for someone concerned with signification, Mandell surprises the reader by calling the public festivals 'strange aspects' of Roman culture (p. 80), or the baths a 'strange indulgence' (p. 85), or one of Henry the Eighth's tournaments 'silly' (p. 115)."[33]

The theoretical framework for a historical analysis of sport on the basis of Eichberg's work has been summarized recently in a book edited by Wilhelm Hopf.[34] Eichberg's "historical behavior research" is placed within the context of other theories. Eric Dunning compares it with the concept proposed by Norbert Elias: as a mode to analyze the "civilizing process."[35] Dunning also points out

that he has not understood it very well . . . The comparison and measurement of processes of development pose difficult methodological issues . . . It is not meaningful as Eichberg does, to extract arbitrarily from their wider development and wider context and to compare particular items such as the "Ballhausspiel" and football . . . since they were separate developments, it is not meaningful to compare them with one another except in relation to wider developments of which they formed part.[36]

Guttmann points to the differences between himself and Eichberg:[37]

According to my opinion we can base the characteristics of modern sports—particularly quantification and the search for ever new records—on the origin and spreading of mathematical—empirical world view. In the social systems of the modern world which differ considerably (USA, USSR, China) we can see a common denominator, i.e., the tendency connected with natural science to quantify every phenomenon. Eichberg's treatment of this explanation is uncharacteristically insufficient. He insists that empirical science could not have been the reason for this change in behavior, as empirical thinking and science have been present in any age.[38]

The argument is wrong. It is not the mere question whether there has been empirical thinking and science in the 17th and 18th century, but the more important question how empirical thinking and science of one age differed from that of another.[39]

From this differentiation we see that what was seen as Eichberg and Guttmann's common position at the beginning of the discussion process can no longer be viewed as so congruent. Guttmann also rejects Dunning and Elias's explanation of the changes in sports in terms of a civilizing process,[40] whereas Eichberg finally defends his method of behavioral research "as the attempt of a systematic method of comparison." In this way he links it to the structural historiography of Michel Foucault.[41]

In more recent times this split between the Guttmann and Eichberg position has become even more blatant. In the Danish publication *Religion og sport*[42] Guttmann points out his unchanged position. For him modern sports contain only a few elements of a worldly religion, although everything is there—the hierarchy, ritual, myths, and values. The ritual was important for people like Coubertin who stressed its role in the Olympic Games, for example, in the joint marching, with flags, the anthems, and so on, all of which promoted the myth of nationalism.[43] Guttmann admitted that his biography of Avery Brundage[44]— which he published after *From Ritual to Record*—could make it appear that he was contradicting himself. In this biography he claimed that Brundage's belief in olympism was religious. Therefore Guttmann now defined religion, ritual, and myth more precisely and thus showed that he accepted some of the ritual in modern sport, though for him it was of only of minor importance compared with record seeking.

In the same Danish journal Ove Korsgaard explains that all of sport is but a present-day ritual. For him modern Protestantism is so devoid of ritual that the modern individual has to find another outlet to satisfy his need for it. Modern sports cater to this need. Therefore, not the Olympic ceremony but rather modern sport as a whole is the ritual. Sport symbolizes the search for progress, for doing things faster than ever before, for rationality. For Korsgaard, sports have a similar ritual function today as dance has in a traditional society. The full argument is translated and reprinted in our reader.[45] In the same periodical[46] Eichberg agrees with Korsgaard and points out the differences between himself and the Danish school and Guttmann in his review of the Brundage biography.[47]

In this discussion process, three side issues should not be overlooked, although they are quite independent from the mainstream of thought. First, there is Richard S. Gruneau and Allen Guttmann's discussion of the origin of modern sports which "can be characterized as a debate between historians influenced primarily by Marx and historians influenced primarily by Weber."[48] Although Guttmann's position has already been described, the sociologist Gruneau states that *From Ritual to Record* "can be regarded as one more contribution to that well-populated tradition of historical and social-scientific work that equates liberalism with objectivity."[49] He terms his own approach Marxist and separates it from neo-

Marxism, Leninism, and Stalinism.[50] Gruneau's main term of reference for the
social analysis of sports is "class inequality," which not only serves as a guide
to the past, but also helps elucidate the present in that the "social definition of
sport is an object of struggles . . . in which what is at stake, *inter alia,* is the
monolytic capacity to impose the legitimate definition of sporting practice and
the legitimate functioning of sporting activity."[51] With regard to Bero Rigauer's
Sport and Work,[52] Rigauer, a "neo-Marxist" is anything but an historian. In
his historical claims he relies on the Polish (*Stalinist* in Gruneau's terms) sociologist Andrzej Wohl whose main historical work sought to prove that the aims
of humankind cannot be realized in the capitalistic system.[53] So scholarship can
be carried out on a Marxian basis without resorting to the dogmatic distortion
of facts.

The second line of thought is intertwined with the first: Both Gruneau and
Guttmann disclaim the ideas of the productive French sociologist Jean-Marie
Bröhm.[54] However, since they use the one English edition available,[55] they do
not take account of the attempt to apply the theories of Michel Foucault, Claude
Lévi-Strauss, and Marcel Mauss to the history of sport.[56] Through these phi-
losophers we have learned that we, as historians, determine what we want to
regard and by choosing certain abstractions, and thereby discarding others, we
influence the current view of the past. This position teaches us that we should
look carefully at our own position to be able to understand the semiotics of sport
and body techniques, the selection of facts and their interpretation through us
as agents in the class struggle. Bröhm also teaches us that one cannot look at
sports in isolation, but whereas Eichberg conjures up any available information,
Bröhm always places it within the context of what is known about the body
(*corps*) and bodily techniques on the whole.[57]

The third line is actively represented in the Association for the Anthropological
Study of Play. This association has produced at least one fine publication annually
since 1974 and has devoted many papers to a discussion of the present state of
modern sports in terms of anthropology. These papers have therefore made us
more aware of the application of anthropological techniques to sports in both
the past and the present. As a consequence, ritual in present-day sports has
become more visible.[58] The vast number of non-European sporting traditions
also shows that developments in modern sports are not automatic, but rather
should always be compared to those of other societies.[59]

When examining the long controversy about the beginning and major features
of sports, it is difficult to state our own position. We have not really been able
to formulate a new theory of the magnitude of those ideas advanced by Guttmann,
Eichberg, Mandell, and Gruneau. Instead, we will attempt a far more modest
approach. Of course, we are aware of Werner Sombart's notion that "a general
history always requires an overall model, good or bad, against which events can
be interpreted. No theory—no history."[60] Yet none of the existing theories is
completely convincing. Perhaps we are traditionalists who believe that many

aspects of Johan Huizinga's *Homo Ludens*[61] are valid, in that certain features in humans tend to change very slowly, if at all. The human animal is ambitious and proud, seeks to gain and maintain power, has sexual drive, and, in many cases, the desire to move. But the changes in sports and physical activities are brought about by changes in human interrelationships by the maturation process, by class relations, by technological inventions, and by changes in what is important for society.

We are also traditional historians in our thinking that fact should precede theory. A theory that cannot accommodate the facts is weak. If too many facts cannot be accommodated, it is time for a new theory. We cannot propose a supertheory that will accommodate all the facts, but in the following chapters we will point out the weaknesses in the other theories. Our selection shows that we have chosen particularly to fill in the gaps. One reason why some of the theories are so weak is that our knowledge of sports history is unevenly distributed over time. Since little has been published recently on medieval and Renaissance sports, very little is known about sports in those eras. Nonetheless, a vast body of knowledge is available. A recent bibliography covers eighty pages.[62]

Another problem is that language may be a limiting factor in dealing with *European* sports history of the past. Of course, adequate coverage of the Middle Ages requires knowledge of Greek, Latin, Italian, Spanish, French, German, and English.[63] In addition, knowledge of Hebrew, Swedish, Portuguese, Provençal, Polish, Russian, and Arabic would be extremely helpful. Since few people know many languages, international cooperation is a necessity. The difficulty of covering all the secondary literature of today presents a somewhat similar problem, in that sports history does not attract a large readership in many countries. Therefore, many valuable detailed studies will not be translated into another and therefore cannot be used so easily. As a result, some works of foreign scholars are presented here in translation. Mandell and Guttmann have introduced, in English, much of what German historical scholarship has produced, but in the recent past[64] the focus of attention for historical studies on sports has shifted to England and France. The translations presented here are from the German and Danish, however.

NOTES

1. Henning Eichberg, "Auf Zoll und Quintlein. Sport und Quantifizierungsprozess in der frühen Neuzeit," *Archiv für Kulturgeschichte* 56 (1974): 141–76.

2. H. Eichberg, *Leistung, Spannung, Geschwindigkeit. Sport und Tanz im gesellschaftlichen Wandel des 18./19. Jahrhunderts* (Stuttgart: Klett-Cotta, 1978). According to the preface, the study was completed between 1973 and December 1975.

3. H. Eichberg, "Spielverhalten und Relationsgesellschaft in West Sumatra. Probleme des interkulturellen Vergleichs und Transfers von Leibesübungen in Südostasien," *Stadion* 11, (1975):1–48; idem, "Den einen Sport gibt es nicht. Das Beispiel West Sumatra. Zur Kritik des olympischen Universalismus," *Zeitschrift für Kulturaustausch* 27 (1977): 72–77; idem, "The Duel. On the Intercultural Comparison of European and

Indonesian Behaviour Patterns'' (Paper presented at the UCLA conference on The Athlete and the Emergence of Modern Spirit, 20–21 June 1980).

4. H. Eichberg, "Geometrie als barocke Verhaltensnorm. Fortifikation und Exercitien," *Zeitschrift f. Hist. Forschung* 4 (1977): 17–50.

5. H. Eichberg, "Zur historisch-kulturellen Relativität des Leistens in Spiel und Sport," *Sportwissenschaft* 6, 1 (1976): 9–34.

6. Richard D. Mandell, "The Invention of the Sports Record," *Stadion* 2, 2 (1976): 250–64.

7. "The Invention of the Sport Record," in Uriel Simri (ed.), *Physical Education and Sport in the Jewish History and Culture*. Proceedings of the Second International Seminar, July 1977 (Netanya: Wingate Institute, 1977), pp. 148–58. It should be noted that *Stadion* always appears months, if not years, after the date on the cover.

8. Walt Rostow, *The Stages of Economic Growth* (Cambridge: Cambridge University Press, 1960). The use of Rostow's work was first suggested by Hilmi Ibrahim, *Sport and Society* (Long Beach, Calif.: Hwong, 1975), p. 117.

9. Maria Kloeren, *Sport und Rekord. Kultursoziologische Untersuchungen zum England des 16. bis 18. Jahrhunderts* (Würzburg: Triltsch, 1935) (reprint Münster: Lit, 1985).

10. H. Eichberg, *Der Weg des Sports in die industrielle Zivilisation* (Baden-Baden: Nomos, 1973); idem, "Der Beginn des modernen Leistens. Terminologische Verschiebungen in der Bewertung von Leibesübungen um 1800," *Sportwissenschaft* 4, 1 (1974): 21–48; idem, "Der Umbruch des Bewegungsverhaltens. Leibesübungen, Spiele und Tänze in der Industriellen Revolution." *Verhaltenswandel in der Industriellen Revolution. Beiträge zur Sozialgeschichte*, A. Nitschke, ed. (Stuttgart: Klett-Cotta, 1975), pp. 118–135; idem, "Schneller, höher, stärker. Der Umbruch in der deutschen Körperkultur um 1900 als Signal gesellschaftlichen Wandels." *Medizin, Naturwisenschaft, Technik und das Zweite Kaiserreich*, G. Mann and R. Winau, eds. (Göttingen: Vandenhoek & Ruprecht, 1977), pp. 259–83.

11. Mandell, *Stadion*, p. 259.

12. Excerpts throughout this volume from Allen Guttmann, *From Ritual to Record: The Nature of Modern Sports*. Copyright © (1978) Columbia University Press, New York. Used by permission. German translation (revised and increased) *Vom Ritual zum Rekord. Das Wesen des modernen Sports* (Schorndorf: Hofmann, 1979).

13. Guttmann, *From Ritual to Record*, p. 16.

14. Ibid.

15. Ibid., p. 85.

16. Akira Ito, "Measuring Strength by Chikaraishi," *History of School Physical Education and Sports Promotion Movement*. Proceedings of the International Seminar of Physical Education and Sports History, Tokyo, 26–30 September 1978, pp. 364–70.

17. Arnd Krüger and Akira Ito, "On the Limitations of Eichberg's and Mandell's Theory of Sports and Their Quantification in View of Chikaraishi," *Stadion* 3, 2 (1977): 244–52.

18. Henning Eichberg, "Recording and Quantifying Performance Is Not Natural—A Reply to Krüger and Ito," *Stadion* 32, (1977): 253–56; Richard D. Mandell: "On the Limitations—A Reply to Krüger and Ito," *Stadion* 3, 2 (1977): p. 257.

19. Eichberg, "Recording and Quantifying Performance," p. 254.

20. Eichberg, *Der Weg des Sports in die industrielle Zivilisation* (Baden-Baden: Nomos, 2nd ed., 1979), pp. 165–75.

21. Ibid., p. 170.

22. *The Athlete and the Emergence of Modern Spirit,* UCLA Center for Medieval and Renaissance Studies, 20–21 June 1980. See Freddi Chiapelli, "Zum Geleit," *Die Anfänge des modernen Sports in der Renaissance,* Arnd Krüger and John McClelland, eds. (London: Arena 1984), pp. 7–8.

23. McClelland, "Einleitung," pp. 9–18.

24. McClelland, "Leibesübungen in der Renaissance und die freien Künste." pp. 85–110.

25. Krüger, "Schwimmen. Der Wandel in der Einstellung zu einer Form der Leibesübungen," pp. 19–42.

26. Allen Guttmann, "Besprechung: Arnd Krüger/John McClelland (Hrsg.): Die Anfänge des modernen Sports in der Renaissance," *Sportwissenschaft* 17, 1 (1987): 98–99.

27. Tomaso Garzoni, *La piazza universale di tutte le professioni del mondo* (Venice: G. B. Somasco, 1587) mentions an acrobat who can jump eight hoops, while Arcangelo Tuccaro, *Trois dialogue de l'exercise de sauter et voltiger en l'air* (Paris: C. de Monstr'oeil, 1599) shows himself jumping ten. Cf. McClelland, "Einleitung," p. 18.

28. William J. Baker, *Sports in the Western World* (Totowa, N.J.: Rowman & Littlefield, 1982), p. vii.

29. Richard D. Mandell, *Sport. A Cultural History* (New York: Columbia University Press, 1984), p. 100.

30. Ibid., p. xvi.

31. James A. Mangan, *Athleticism in the Victorian and Edwardian Public School* (Cambridge: Cambridge University Press, 1981); idem, *The Games Ethnic and Imperialism* (Harmondsworth: Viking Press, 1986) (which, of course, Mandell could not have known at the time of writing his book).

32. Roland Renson, "Leibesübungen der Bürger und Bauern im Mittelalter," *Geschichte der Leibesübungen,* vol. 3/1, Horst Ueberhorst, ed. (Berlin: Bartels & Wernitz, 1980), pp. 97–144.

33. Stephen H. Hardy, "Book Review. Mandell, Richard D.: Sport: A Cultural History," *Journal of Sport History* 12, 2 (1985): 169–73.

34. Wilhelm Hopf (ed.), *Die Veränderung des Sports ist gesellschaftlich. Diskussionsband* (Münster: Lit, 1986). (The volume contains many shortened papers by Eichberg up to 1977, and other authors discuss them.)

35. Eric Dunning, "The 'Civilizing Process' and the Development of Modern Football," pp. 42–50. Cf. in more detail Norbert Elias and Eric Dunning, *Quest for Excitement. Sport and Leisure in the Civilizing Process* (Oxford: Basil Blackwell, 1986).

36. Dunning, "The 'Civilizing Process,' " p. 46f.

37. See Guttmann, *From Ritual to Record* Eichberg, *Der Weg des Sports,* pp. 135–37.

38. See Guttmann, *From Ritual to Record* Eichberg, "Geometrie als barocke Verhaltensnorm," p. 47.

39. Allen Guttmann, "Stellungnahme zu Henning Eichbergs Auffassung des Problems historischen Wandels," *Die Veränderung des Sports,* pp. 169.

40. Ibid., p. 169.

41. H. Eichberg, "Was wird? Ein grünes Nachwort," *Der Weg des Sports,* pp. 271–84.

42. Ejgil Jespersen, "Religion og Sport," *Centring* 7, 1 (1986).

43. Allen Guttmann, "Olympisme i glimt," *Centring* 7, 1 (1986): 35–45.

44. Allen Guttmann, *The Games Must Go on. Avery Brundage and the Olympic Movement* (New York: Columbia University Press, 1984).

45. Ove Korsgaard, "Sport som relogiøs praksis," *Centring* 7, 1 (1986): 57–67.

46. H. Eichberg, "Det sanselige i at korsfæste kødet," *Centring* 7, 1 (1986): 68–81.

47. H. Eichberg, "Religionsgeschichte des Olympismus" (Book review of Allen Guttmann, *The Games Must Go on), Stadion* 10 (1984): 257–59. (This volume was published in 1987.)

48. Allen Guttmann, "Book review. Gruneau, Richard. Class, Sports, and Social Development," *Journal of Sport History* 11, 1 (1984): 97–99. Cf. Richard S. Gruneau, "Freedom and Constraint: The Paradoxes of Play, Games, and Sports," *Journal of Sport History* 7, 3 (1980): 68–86.

49. Richard S. Gruneau, *Class, Sports, and Social Development* (Amherst, Mass.: University of Massachusetts Press, 1983), p. 47.

50. Ibid., p. 48.

51. Ibid., p. 53. Gruneau takes up the argument of Gramsci through Pierre Bourdieu in this instance.

52. Bero Rigauer, *Sport und Arbeit* (Frankfurt: Suhrkamp 1969). It was translated into English by Allen Guttmann as *Sport and Work* (New York: Columbia University Press, 1981).

53. Ibid., p. 7 n. 1 (German edition) relates to A. Wohl, "Die gesellschaftlich-historischen Grundlagen des bürgerlichen Sports," *Wiss. Zeitschrift der DHfK Leipzig* 6, 1 (1964): 5–93 (reprinted with some alterations as a monograph: Köln: Pahl-Rugenstein, 1973). The quote is from ibid., p. 186.

54. He is the author of more than ten monographs and the editor of *Quel Corps?* Since 1975 he has written almost half of the thirty-three issues. We would regard as his main works his *Corps et politique* (Paris: Ed. Univ., 1975); *Sociologie politique du sport* (Paris: Ed. Univ., 1976); and *Le mythe olympique* (Paris: Bourgois, 1981).

55. Jean-Marie Bröhm, *Sport. A Prison of Measured Time. Essays by Jean-Marie Bröhm* (London: Ink Links, 1978).

56. J. M. Bröhm, "Pouvoir Corps. Interview avec Michel Foucault," *Quel Corps?* 1, 2 (1975): 2–5.; idem, "La critique du sport. Les enjeux actuels," *Quel Corps?* 11,30/ 31 (1986): 2–17.

57. All of his journal serves as a point in matter with its sometimes drastic caricatures, but his theoretical position is best stated in idem, "Le corps: un paradigme de la modernité?" *Actions et Recherches Sociales* 18, 1 (1985): 15–38.

58. For example, Scott Kilmer, "Sport as Ritual. A Theoretical Approach," *The Study of Play. Problems and Prospects,* D. A. Lancy, B. A. Tindall, eds. (West Point, N.Y.: Leisure Press, 1977), pp. 44–49; A. W. Miracle, "Voluntary Ritual as Recreational Therapy. A Study of Baths at Hot Springs, Arkansas," *The Many Faces of Play,* K. Blanchard, ed. (Champaign, Ill.: Human Kinetics, 1986), pp. 164–71; K. Blanchard and A. Cheska, "The Meaning of Sport: A Cultural Approach," *The Anthropology of Sport,* Blanchard and Cheska, eds. (South Hadley, Mass.: Bergin & Garvey, 1985), pp. 29–62; B. Megen, "Reisman Redux: Football as Work, Play, Ritual and Metaphor," *Play as Context,* A. Cheska, ed. (West Point, N.Y.: Leisure Press, 1981), pp. 106–16; A. O. Dunleavy and A. W. Miracle, "Sport: An Experimental Setting for the Development of a Theory of Ritual," pp. 118–26; J. A. Beran, "The Iowa Girls' High School Basketball Tournament Viewed as an Institutionalized Ritual," pp. 149–57; J. H. Duthie, "Athletics: The Ritual of a Technological Society?" *Play and Culture,* H. B. Schwartzmann,

ed. (West Point, N.Y.: Leisure Press, 1980), pp. 91–98; A. W. Miracle, "School Spirit as a Ritual By-Product: A View from Applied Anthropology," *Play and Culture,* pp. 98–103; J. C. Harris, "Sport and Ritual: A Macroscopic Comparison of Form," *The Paradoxes of Play,* J. Loy, ed. (West Point, N.Y.: Leisure, 1982), pp. 205–14; S. Birrell, "Sport as Ritual: Interpretations from Durkheim to Goffman," *Social Forces* 60, 2 (1981): 354–76; M. Deegan and M. Stein, "American Drama and Ritual: Nebraska Football," *Int. Rev. of Sport Sociol.* 13 (1978): 31–42.

59. The Proceedings are full of examples, particularly of North American Indians, but also of examples from Africa and Asia. Eichberg's choice of Sumatra becomes all the more random by the richness of examples.

60. Quoted by S. Hardy, "Book Review," p. 170.

61. Johan Huizinga, *Homo Ludens* (Boston: Beacon, 1955); idem, *Homo Ludens* (Reinbek: Rowohlt Taschenbuch, 1960).

62. Arnd Krüger and John McClelland, "Ausgewählte Bibliographie zu Leibesübungen und Sport in der Renaissance," *Die Anfänge des modernen Sports in der Renaissance,* pp. 132–80.

63. John Marshall Carter, "Communication," *Journal of Sport History* 11, 1 (1984): 138–39.

64. Arnd Krüger, "Linee di sviluppo della storiografia sportiva nella Republica Federale Tedesca," *Itinerari di storia dell' educazione fisica e dello sport,* G. Gori and R. Isidori Frasca, eds. (Bologna: Patron 1987), pp. 99–112; idem, Bertrand During, "Histoires des activités physiques et sportives," *Science et Motricité* 1, 2 (1987): 35–43; idem, "The Historiography of Sport in Germany," *Physical Education Review* 10, 2 (1987): 145–51.

2

The New Sport History

DONALD PARKERSON

Fifteen years ago the first issue of the *Journal of Sport History* was published by the North American Society for Sport History. Its purpose was to provide a forum for the publication of articles and papers in this new field of scholarly inquiry and to stimulate further research in this area. Since then a number of other fine journals have commenced publication, and the field of sport history has emerged as an important subdiscipline of historical analysis.

Like all "new" substantive areas of history, sport history has embraced a wide diversity of methodologies and chronological periods. Indeed, although this diversity has demonstrated the wide applications of sport to an understanding of the past, it has at the same time become almost overwhelming to the uninitiated. Even a cursory reading of the *Journal of Sport History*'s special review issue commemorating ten years of publication illustrates the geographical, chronological, and ideological controversies inherent in this new field.[1]

The problem here is that in a search for diversity and uniqueness, the field is in danger of losing sight of the essential commonalities of sport and how these common themes transcend the rather narrow ideological and disciplinary boundaries that are all too familiar to historians.

Although this chapter will not attempt to synthesize this growing field, it will suggest a new theoretical approach for sport history which will emphasize commonality over peculiarity and will draw sport history directly into the wider substantive concerns of the historical discipline, especially the so-called new history. In short, we will discuss the broad contours of the new history generally and discuss how sport history relates to it.

THE NEW HISTORY

In the last two decades the field of historical inquiry has undergone some rather interesting changes. Included in these changes has been the emergence of a variety of new histories including the new economic, political, and social history. Basically, these new histories are an interdisciplinary form of historical analysis drawing both substantive and methodological insights from areas that were traditionally seen as part of history's sister disciplines of demography, sociology, and economics.

If we were to compare the new histories with more traditional forms of historical inquiry, we would find five basic differences: the population examined, new historical questions, new theoretical approaches, new sources of data and techniques, and the application of the scientific method to historical problems.

Perhaps the most important characteristic of the new history is an interest in the lives of the common folk of the past rather than the handful of elites on which historians traditionally have focused. This interest in everyday people which emerged partly out of the political and social conflict of the 1960s has encouraged historians to examine groups which until recently have been ignored. These include women, ethnic groups, blacks, working people, and the poor. By revealing their stories, the new history has fundamentally altered the discipline of history itself.

This simple shift in focus from the elites to the participants and audiences within sport has had a dramatic impact on the field itself. By examining the lives, families, class, ethnicity, gender, and social mobility of sport figures we can determine the impact of sport in a broader social and economic context. The role of ethnic groups and blacks in contemporary sport and the success or failure that these groups had in the past reveal a great deal about the sport itself and provide a mirror to examine the issues and changes within the broader society.

This interest in the lives of the common folk has led new historians to a broader conceptualization of the discipline of history and has encouraged historians to assume an interdisciplinary perspective. As a result, we have seen the blossoming of a variety of new historical fields. Of particular interest to the sport historian is the emergence of the fields of social and geographical mobility, as well as family history. Here the focus of the researcher moves away from the sport figures themselves toward their social and economic *milieux*. Perhaps the most fundamental question concerning the participants in sport in the past is who they were. What was their social and economic class, and did it change as a result of their involvement in sport? Sport, of course, was much more than a game, and it could have been an avenue of social and economic mobility which eroded the rigid contours of hierarchical societies. Documentation of that mobility (or lack of it) once again places sport history firmly in the context of the new social history.

In terms of theoretical orientation, the new historians generally embrace the nomothetic approach to history rather than the idiographic perspective, which is more typical of traditional histories. The nomothetic approach attempts to discover regular patterns within the historical drama and then to generalize findings based on a particular group to the larger group under consideration. In the context of the new sport history we might examine the experiences of a particular community's soccer club or baseball team. But rather than focusing on the uniqueness of that soccer or baseball club, the new historian would examine these groups as a clue to the development of other clubs in other areas or at other times.

This micro examination of the social mobility of participants, of audiences, and of the role of different ethnic groups and classes within the sport might provide unique insights into the sport in general and further clarify the role of sport in social and economic change.

This theoretical approach clearly is a fundamental divergence from more traditional approaches to history. Once again the focus is on the commonality of experience rather than the peculiarities of a group, individual, or team. Moreover, by assuming this theoretical posture the new sport historian will demonstrate the general development of sport rather than the idiosyncratic aspects of an obscure team or individual.

New historians have also begun to examine a variety of new sources which traditionally have been seen as outside the purview of history itself. Once again, the new sport historian can benefit from these kinds of sources. Since traditional historians typically tell us little about the lives of everyday people, they have often avoided a wealth of data which new historians have found very helpful. Census manuscripts, for example, might be useful in examining contemporary sport figures and will allow us insights into his or her family structure, wealth holding, ethnicity, kin structure, and general level of education and literacy. These records are also useful to examine the migration patterns of the sport figure and his family and can provide some unique insights into his or her social milieu.

Genealogical records, which are readily available in most research libraries, can provide some important longitudinal data on the family of the sport figure, whereas city directories can yield some important information into the institutional framework of sport teams themselves. Here suggestions as to the power structures within a community are available and waiting for the assertive researcher to sort them out in detail.

In addition, a wide array of other records can provide the researcher with some important insights into sport figures and their social and economic environment. A systematic investigation of the Bayeux Tapestry, for example, has revealed the important role of sport in medieval society,[2] whereas a prosopographic investigation of *The Canterbury Tales* or other records might reveal something of the place of sport in other periods. Court records dating to the Middle Ages and earlier have provided insights into the nature and role of sport in the past, and for more modern periods, marriage and birth records, tax records, naturalization records, obituaries and probate records can yield a wealth of information on sport figures.

In order to utilize these data effectively, new historians have embraced techniques of nominal record linkage. Basically, these techniques allow the researcher to bring together a variety of sources of data relating to individuals (in this case sport figures) in order to develop a more textured portrait of those individuals. For example, the historian might search institutional records and then examine marriage and birth records, census manuscripts, and city directories to discover additional information about a group of people. This "collective biographic" approach can be very useful and provide important comparisons of groups of sport figures. Moreover, these techniques draw the sport figures into the larger historical context.

Finally, since the new historians frequently examine large groups of individuals in the past, they often employ descriptive and inferential statistics, and sophisticated sampling designs; they use computers and software packages like SPSS-X or SAS to analyze and organize their data.[3]

Underlying each of the differences between the new history and more traditional forms of history are attitudes toward the scientific method. Although many volumes have been devoted to the explication of this type of inquiry, the scientific method can be summarized in five steps.

The first step is the identification of characteristics (or variables) to be studied. These include measures of things one should understand, called independent variables, as well as those to be elucidated, called dependent variables. The new sport historian might want to understand the prospects (dependent variable) of a sport figure with information on his or her race, parental support, type of sport, gender, and so on (independent variables).

The second step is the generation of a hypothesis or series of hypotheses concerning relationships between these factors. The researcher might argue that the success of sport figures during a particular period was directly related to their parents' support of their activities at an early age, their fathers' success as an athlete, the kinds of formal coaching they received at a critical age, and so forth.

Once these relationships are stated explicitly, we move to the third step of the scientific method: the testing of these hypothesized relationships against reality as measured by our data (the systematic evidence collected from the representative group). We then evaluate our results (often using standard statistical methods or qualitative techniques) and attempt to generalize our findings to other athletes at other times or places. Finally, we suggest the importance of our work, note problems in our research, and discuss other hypotheses that have emerged from our analysis.

In short, the scientific method tests our ideas in a rigorous manner with each step in the analysis explicitly detailed.

Table 2.1
Differences between the Traditional and New History

	Traditional	New
Researcher's values are identified.	Yes	Yes
Researcher develops hypotheses.	Yes	Yes
Researcher outlines method of testing these hypotheses.	No	Yes
Researcher generates results relating to these hypotheses.	Yes	Yes

Table 2.1 outlines some of the differences and similarities in the approach between traditional and new historians. While they are quite similar (though traditional historians may not see their work in these terms and new historians might argue that traditional historians do not generate hypotheses), one critical difference is clear. This involves the replication of research, the idea that the work of one scholar can be repeated exactly to determine whether similar or conflicting results might be generated. When replication is not possible (usually because no precise methodology has been presented), researchers must begin anew at each stage of inquiry to investigate the phenomena under question. Traditional history is seldom replicated simply because methods of inquiry, data collection, and analysis are seldom explicit. The traditional historian might footnote that someone said something about something, but this is only a start. If the new historian used this same device, he or she would suggest a finding and then simply refer to the census volume as evidence of that finding. Although footnoting is critically important, it only identifies a source and cannot be a substitute for the clarification of method—which is a very different thing indeed.

But why even bother with the new history when more traditional forms of historical inquiry have been the mainstay of the profession for well over a century. There is, of course, no simple answer to this question. What has become clear in recent years, however, is that these new approaches have provided us with an important complement to the more traditional forms of history. Certainly the sport biography, for example, will remain an important idiom of this field, as it will in other areas of history. But the sport biography focuses on the uniqueness of individuals (a certain figure was important *because* he or she was unique) and says little about how some of his or her less successful contemporaries fared in and out of the game. By augmenting the biography with what new historians call the collective biography, the research can begin to focus not only on the uniqueness of an individual, but also on the themes that were common to most players at that time. In this way both individual and group processes become clearer.

Similarly, the new sport history will begin to resolve some of the historiographical dilemmas which the field must resolve. A good example is the debate surrounding the question of "ritual and record" which provides the central theme of this volume. In his analysis of the development of sports in the "modern" era, Allen Guttmann has argued that sport emerged in tandem with the technology (and inherent quantification) of modern industrial society.[5] While this argument, based primarily on vague symbolic evidence, has intrigued many scholars of post-industrial society, it suggests that sport had little continuity with its medieval or ancient past. In short, this methodological approach distorted the essential commonality of sport history demonstrated so clearly in the pages of this volume.

This is not to argue that Guttmann's work is without merit. It is merely to suggest that, by assuming a traditional, idiographic, theoretical perspective on sport history, he has tended to ignore a millennium of sport development as well as decades of historical analysis devoted to sport.

The history of the family once had a similar historiographical dilemma. Not too many years ago sociologists and historians argued quite forcefully that our contemporary nuclear family was the result of powerful anomic influences of modern society which had torn asunder the typically extended household of the past. As society became more modern, it was argued, the "traditional" household vanished leaving contemporary people isolated from their warm familial moorings. But the research of new social historian Peter Laslett and his associates at Cambridge during the late 1960s and early 1970s demonstrated very clearly that as early as the sixteenth century most families were nuclear and not extended.[6] In short, when traditional ideas about the family were actually tested rigorously (rather than simply invented to fit a particular argument), we found a very different situation and were forced to reconsider the supposed decline of the modern family.

The parallel to sport history is direct and important. By assuming a narrow idiographic historical perspective and by garnering evidence that clearly cannot be replicated and tested, we may misdirect the field and do a disservice to the emerging discipline of sport history itself.

Another problem with Guttmann's analysis of the development of modern sport involves a basic violation of another tenet of the scientific method as embraced by new historians—the concept of falsifiability. Early in his work Guttmann argues that there are seven "distinguishing characteristics of modern sport as contrasted with those of previous eras"[7] (formation of hypotheses): secularization, equality of opportunity, specialization of roles, rationalization, bureaucratic organization, quantification, and the quest for records.

Working in the traditional mode of historical inquiry, Guttmann garners evidence to support these major contentions but plays only lip-service to the possibility of conflicting evidence. He notes, for example, that "In actual practice there are numerous inequalities" in contemporary sport, but he suggests that these are due more to the "contemporary state of affairs"[8] than to a negation of his theoretical model. Similarly, he rejects the possibility of equality "in medieval times" (+ or − 500 years?), noting that "jousts and tournaments were limited to the nobility.''[9] But Guttmann offers no citation or evidence for this rather broad assertion.

If we examine Guttmann's theoretical approach in a logical framework, we can see the basic problem. The following list shows the intellectual matrix in his conceptualization of the relationship between modernity and equality in sport.

	Modern	Premodern
Equality	a	b
No Equality	c	d

Guttmann focuses on cells *a* and *d* (with little evidence) while ignoring cells *b* and *c* entirely. In so doing he has weakened his overall argument by violating the notion of falsifiability; that is, he presents evidence and data on both sides of an issue and then determines the validity of his hypothesis. Unlike a member of a debating club, historians must present all the evidence and then make their conclusions based on that evidence.

Indeed, any historian with the rudiments of professional training can garner evidence to support just about any hypothesis. Unfortunately, some scholars tend to ignore conflicting evidence which seems to detract from their overall thesis.

A couple of examples might clarify this point. Was baseball premodern before Jackie Robinson broke the color line in professional baseball? (Perhaps barbaric is a more appropriate description.) Do most sports today remain premodern because there are no women players in most of the major professional sports? (Sexist yes, but premodern?) How many polo players are poor? What is the socioeconomic status of professional golfers? Certainly no poor folks here. These are just a few examples of rampant age, gender, class, and race inequalities within sport today which are apparently unimportant in Guttmann's scheme of things. Similarly, what of the alleged inequality of sport within medieval society? Guttmann's anecdotal and secondary evidence simply will not do here. A handful of references to support this notion simply reduces ''premodern'' sport to a parody of itself.

The point here is that cases of premodern equality and modern inequality within sport certainly existed. But it simply will not do to ignore, or dismiss as unimportant, evidence that seems to conflict with a stated hypothesis. Indeed, this rationale can be applied with equal vigor to Guttmann's other six characteristics of modern sport.

How might the new sport historians handle the dilemma presented above? They would systematically examine all the available comparable evidence (not just references) from all four of the cells depicted in the listing. They would then determine the *degree* to which ''modern sport'' differed from its premodern forms. In this way the field of sport history will begin to move from anecdotal polemics to a systematic examination of basic historiographical questions.

This, of course, will be no easy task, but it can and must be done. As new sport historians begin to examine new sources of data and systematically investigate the social, political, and economic milieu of sport history, new answers to old questions (as well as new questions) will emerge. The chapters in this volume reveal this important new direction and certainly will nurture the field of sport history in the future.

NOTES

1. See *Journal of Sport History* 10, no. 1, (Spring 1983). Special Review Issue.

2. John M. Carter (ed.), *The Bayeux Tapestry As A Social Document* (Springfield, MA: Ginn, 1985).

3. There are numerous works devoted to statistical analysis and the use of computer package programs for historians. For a brief introduction to the use of statistics, see D. H. Parkerson, "Statistics and Consumers: Reading Quantitative History," *OAH Newsletter* (February 1984). (The author will furnish a reprint of this article.) For computers, see N. Nie et al., *SPSS-X* (New York: McGraw-Hill, 1984) or J. Helwig et al., *SAS* (Raleigh, N.C.: SAS Institute, 1979).

4. An excellent introduction to the scientific method is Kenneth R. Hoover, *The Elements of Social Scientific Thinking*, 4th ed., (New York: St. Martin's Press, 1988).

5. Allen Guttmann, *From Ritual to Record* (New York: Columbia University Press, 1978).

6. Peter Laslett, *The World We Have Lost* (Cambridge: Cambridge University Press, 1968).

7. Guttmann, *From Ritual to Record*, p. 15.

8. Ibid., p. 26.

9. Ibid., p. 30.

3

The Record of the Ritual: The Athletic Records of Ancient Egypt

WOLFGANG DECKER

Following the research of R. D. Mandell and H. Eichberg, Allen Guttmann postulated the sport record as the direct opposite of ritual in his work *From Ritual to Record*. Ritual was supposedly the distinctive feature of ancient sport, whereas modern sport is characterized by records.[1] Previously, Mandell had hypothesized that the record was an invention of the progressive-industrial England of the second half of the nineteenth century.[2] The historical and social predispositions had already been present, so that the origins could have been seen in the eighteenth century.[3] According to the definition of this American historian, who based his work on Eichberg's research,[4] the sport record was the mark of a democratic industrial society in which highly competitive sport mirrored a performance-oriented society. Its existence was bound to such social values as organization, planning, competition, bureaucratization, quantification, standardization, norming, codification, and technical advances.[5] In other words, sport was a phenomenon that developed only under the very particular social-historical conditions present in eighteenth- and nineteenth-century England.

This thesis has been criticized by Arnd Krüger and Akira Ito based on seventeenth- to early twentieth-century Japanese weightlifting (*Chikaraishi*) records to point out the universal and "natural" development and distribution of the record.[6]

With all due respect to the adherents of the thesis of the modern notion of the record, they should have had a more profound knowledge of antiquity and acknowledged the example cited by Krüger and Ito.[7] They have translated the inscription on the tombstone of C. Apuleius Diocles, which records the unsurpassed career of a charioteer in the Roman Circus. The inscription lists all his victories in competitions held over nearly twenty-four years; in modern terms, this can only be called a record list. This was not a singular occurrence, but rather only a major example illustrating how, in the second century, enormous sums of money could be won in sporting chariot races.[8]

None of the above authors deal in any length with ancient Egypt.[9] In addition, we should note that I. Weiler, a major expert on sport in antiquity, quite naturally links "records" of antiquity to modern world records.[10]

Not withstanding all the differences in social and technical conditions between the ancient and modern world, ancient Greek sports achieved a considerable perfection, which coincided with a noticeable social recognition of gymnastics and agonistics in public life. Oddly, only a very few performances were actually recorded in times and distances or in other quantifiable data. This peculiarity alone however, does not, justify the conclusion that "records" were nonexistent (i.e., the registration of a thus far unreached athletic performance). Frequently, victory lists noted the number of victories scored by a particular athlete. Normally, victories were noted only in first-class athletic meets, the so-called pan-Hellenic festivals such as the Olympic, Pythian, Isthmic, and Nemean Games. As these inscriptions were often placed at the site of the victories (e.g., Olympia[11] or Delphi), the visitor's acknowledgment of such lists of athletic accomplishments created a type of qualitative listing of the results. These lists are somewhat akin to "records" in the modern sense. These athletic performances were quite consciously accepted as records when a victor claimed he was the first of his polis or region to have won a particular event in a certain major festival.[12] This custom had already begun in the fifth century B.C.[13] and became more frequent in fourth-century epigrams.[14]

In the Roman imperial period the use of such inscriptions expanded. According to J. Ebert: "The increasing professionalization (more personal ambition to be a specialist among the specialists) is the major reason for the obvious striving for records."[15] J. Ebert places the "invention" of the "I (ego)" notion in philosophy, politics, and art on the same level as the beginning of the Greek idea of the record in the fifth century.[16] Sophistics, democracy, and the art of portraying are closely linked culturally to the emphasis on supreme individual performance, abstracted as the "record." It fits neatly into this pattern that today the Greek word *arete* is no longer simply translated as "virtue" (lat. *virtus*) but as "performance."[17]

The purpose of this chapter, however, is not to discuss the notion of the athletic record in classical antiquity. Rather, as has been previously attempted[18]— it is to define more closely the sports record in pharaonic high culture. The aim here is not to destroy the previously mentioned thesis. On the contrary, it is hoped that their chapter will renew the discussion on a more profound level.

To understand the sources for the Egyptian "records," it is necessary to mention some basic information about ancient Egyptian history. It will become obvious that conditions in the Eighteenth Dynasty were particularly conducive to the development of the sports record.

The Egyptian king as ruler stood as guarantor of the well-being of the country and his people. He was the intermediator between men and the gods, and he helped to sustain the proper world order with his invincibility in war and his prowess as a hunter.[19] Victories over enemies who threatened the very existence of Egypt and the successful hunting of wild animals were the pharaoh's chief correlative functions. From the beginning of Egyptian history the warlike nature of the king, which went back to his prehistoric role as ruler of the tribe, was closely related to his athletic prowess.[20] The dogma of the kingship which determined the official role model could be influenced by historical powers. For obvious reasons it was thoroughly revised at the beginning of the New Kingdom. This was at the time when the Egyptians protected their independence and defended themselves against the Hyksos who were the first foreign rulers to invade the Nile Valley. E. Hornung has dealt extensively with the role model of the kings in the Eighteenth Dynasty and concludes that the new royal self-image was characterized by the Pharaoh's duty to enlarge the existing condition.[21]

This "dynamic element"[22] of the Egyptian kingdom did not relate solely to the borders of the country, which had to be moved forward due to the traumatic experience of the Hyksos era. Among the duties of a new pharaoh was the obligation to surpass the deeds and performances of his predecessors. "This is the distinctive feature and fascinating in the New Kingdom that it esteems highly not only order and systematization but also the unique and the new. The kings opened new paths, wanted to surpass their predecessors and felt themselves as somebody who would never be surpassed by anybody in any other time."[23] So it can be shown that the royal tomb was enlarged from modest beginnings to ever increasing dimensions until, finally, in the Ramesside time, it was moved more than 100 meters into solid rock.[24] The individual arts of the tomb were increased over the number of their predecessors. In the middle of the Eighteenth Dynasty the number had reached thirteen.[25] The height and width of the corridors and the number of doors were increased.[26] Even the poles on which the images of the gods were carried at processions were lengthened.[27] Festivities were extended by several days. The Opet Festival reached a "record length"[28] of twenty-seven days under Ramses III (Nineteenth Dynasty). The enormous construction activity at the temples—which would be considered hectic by our standards—was characteristic for the kings of the Nineteenth Dynasty and was based on the "law of enlargement of the existing" which provided its legitimization.[29]

This ideological attitude of royalty vis-à-vis performance is reflected in the fixation on formulas that emphasized the uniqueness of particular actions.[30] For Hornung it was the basis for "the impressive dynamism of the ancient Egyptian culture."[31]

The creative impetus of the kings did not stop at athletic performances. The Eighteenth Dynasty marked the peak of the development of the athletic pharaoh. The sources emphasize that a number of kings were excellent archers who shot their arrows from the moving chariot of one axle drawn by two horses, precisely

Table 3.1
Development of the Royal Archery Records in the Eighteenth Dynasty

King	Thickness of Target	Performance Penetration of Arrow	Peculiari- ties	Spec- tators	Source
Tuthmosis III	3 fingers	3 handwidths	---	yes	QT 14
Amenophis II	3 fingers	3 handwidths	several times	yes	QT 19
Amenophis II	3 fingers	7/9 arrow	competition	yes	QT 20
Amenophis II	1 hand- width	all through	4 targets, each time, first try		QT 17
Tutanchamun	x fingers	all through	x targets	yes	Urk.IV 2047

T= Decker (ed.), Quellentexte, 1975.
Urk.= Helck (ed.), Urkunden der 18. Dynastie

into their targets. This performance, which in itself was quite amazing, can be seen as even more astonishing when we consider that their arrows went straight through the target which was of pure copper. This complex athletic skill was recorded as early as the Eighteenth Dynasty, after the Egyptians had learned the use of chariot and horses from the Hyksos.[32] The invaders also brought the new composite bow,[33] which allowed unprecedented flexibility. As the archer warrior, the pharaoh represented the model of his times. As athletic archer, he could demonstrate this skill, and his sport became the royal favorite in the New Kingdom. The targets were very peculiar: they resembled an oxskin, stretched over the copper frame. In various parts of the Mediterranean these copper ingots, have been found among the cargo of a ship that sank off the Turkish south coast in the thirteenth century B.C., that is, in the times of the Nineteenth Dynasty, still a part of the New Kingdom.[34] This much sought-after trade item, which was offered in the Mediterranean ports, was about 60 by 45 cm.

Four of the known texts from the Eighteenth Dynasty contain quantifiable performances (see Table 3.1). For example, Tuthmosis III shot at a target three fingers thick with such vigor that the arrow pierced through three handwidths.[35] This performance was equaled by that of his son Amenophis II on a shooting stela (Figure 3.1):

The big target of copper form the copperland three fingers thick. The Strong pierced it with several arrows and made them stick out at the back side three handwidths. He was shooting and hit the target each time, the hero, the lord of power. His majesty undertook this task in the face of all the population.[36]

By repeating this performance several times, the unusual feat of the predecessor became a normality and was thus no longer exceptional. The record was also surpassed by Amenophis himself. A destroyed inscription of Medamud explains that he pierced the target of the same thickness in the first attempt by seven-ninths of the length of the arrow. [37] But this was not enough; at a special occasion he performed a record never achieved again. On a "northern shooting range" he shot through four targets, each one a handwidth thick (i.e., four fingers completely), so that the arrows dropped to the ground on the other side of the target. "This was a deed which was never achieved before, of which one has not heard in any report."[38]

This record may have been broken by Tutankhamen. One of the inscriptions mentions that the pharaoh who died quite young shot through a target and established a record.[39] These proofs over so many years are not the result of chance, they reflect the dogma of the kingdom under the new rule, that is, improvement over previously attained performances.

Let us now investigate whether the term *record* really fits.[40] The basic idea of a record is that an athletic performance that has never been achieved before takes place in the presence of witnesses and it is measured with exactitude. As exterior conditions are known and the implements standardized, the performance can be repeated at any given location and at any given time, or it can even be surpassed. At the demonstrations of royal archery skills, spectators were present,[41] and the performance was measured in several ways: the thickness of the target, the depth at which the arrow pierced through the target, and, in one case, the difference of the distances of the targets from one another. The records minutes were published. Even the necessity of standardizing the implements was fulfilled. The copper ingots which served as targets were almost identical in size, weight, and thickness,[42] if you consider the technical possibilities of the middle of the second millennium B.C. In any case, they were standardized. We should forget the modern notion that a measurement is exact only if measured up to two digits behind the point. Ancient Egypt was a land of bureaucracy par excellence as it provided exact lists of activities, both athletic and others. It can therefore be termed the prototype of performance measurement. The scribe sitting at the harvest site, taking note of every grain, is a repeated motif in old Egyptian harvest scenes.[43] Against this background, the king's athletic performance represents an abstraction of the quantifying habit.

The athletic competition is the traditional, though not the exclusive, form for achieving a record. Because of the dogma of the pharaoh, the competitive form was impossible because competition per se[44] would have cast doubt on the superiority of the king and on the uniqueness of his performance. The very idea of a competition allowing an open comparison of performances in which the winner would be determined would have been irreconcilable with the very nature of the king who was the guarantor of the existing world order.[45] Therefore, the only performances with which the king could compare himself were his own or those of his predecessors. As a result, competition between kings

Figure 3.1
Archery Stella from the Third Pylon at Karnak

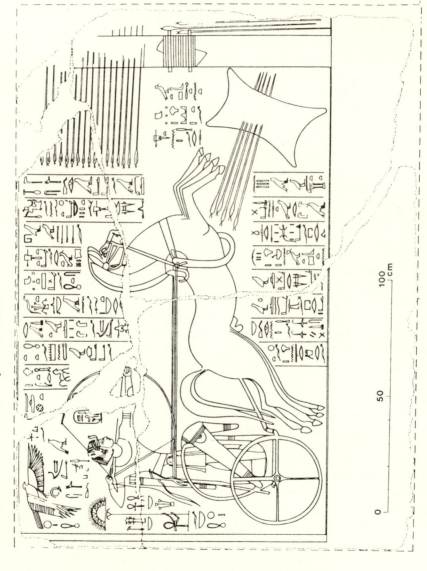

Source: Peter Der Manuelian, *Hildesheimer Ägyptologische Beiträge* (Studies in the Reign of Amenophis II). Vol. 26. Hildesheim: Gerstenberg, 1987.

was a competition by correspondence. Allen Guttmann considered this the very idea of the record: "What is a 'record' in the modern sense? The notion contains a 'genial abstraction' which permits competition between the living and the dead."[46] In ancient Egypt this "genial abstraction" was part of the royal dogma; yet it was possible as a construction and possibly for the first time in human history.

The Egyptian notion of the record gains even more weight through the following consideration: is it not self-evident that one can shoot an arrow through a copper ingot? The respective shooting experiments were repeated at the Cologne University of Sport.[47] Therefore, it could well be that the Egyptian sources and texts did not exaggerate very much.[48] As the Egyptian notion of history does not have historic truth at its center, but the desired image of the world order,[49] the inscriptions such as those relating to the bow and arrow records had the ability to influence the order of the world in a magical way, as the omnipotent king is playing his customary superb role. It can be concluded that the notion of the record was deeply rooted in the Eighteenth Dynasty, as it could not be based on facts. The creation of such records seems to be based on pure imagination, which can only have their roots in cultural phenomena. In other words, the form of the record had to be so common in Ancient Egypt that it is reflected in their ideas.

Conditions were favorable in the Eighteenth Dynasty for recording performances; at the same time performances were also emphasized in the private lives of the citizens. The newly emerging class of the charioteer-warriors, who were the backbone of the state and who considered themselves the elite, were performance oriented, as can be seen in the biographies on their tombs.[50] This has been known to Egyptologists for many years and need not be explained here.[51] The social changes that favored the charioteer-warrior over the traditional elite of the scribes can be explained from the historic context of the time. The political emphasis was on liberation from the Hyksos, which could be achieved only through military might, and not by virtues of the old canon.

The royal arrow shooting of the Eighteenth Dynasty had a ritual aspect in spite of its athletic elements and the pleasure which it represented for the pharaoh. It was part of the ideology of the kingdom and had the character of royal propaganda. It is obvious that penetrating the Asian copper ingot (its origin is specially noted on the sphinx stela of Amenophis II) with the arrow was a symbolic action, a ritual to safeguard the order of the world. It may be pointed out that in this case the record was part of the ritual. To relate the dichotomy of Allen Guttmann's *From Ritual to Record* to ancient Egyptian times, one would have to strip the two notions of their polarization. The "record of the ritual" would raise the question in this respect, whether or not modern records are only a new edition of an old theme, a "reinvention" as R. D. Mandell accepts for other aspects of modern sports which reached their summit in antiquity.[52]

NOTES

This chapter was first published as "Der Rekord des Rituals. Zum sportlichen Rekord im Alten Ägypten," in: *Sport zwischen Eigenständigkeit und Selbstbestimmung. Pädagogische und historische Beiträge aus der Sportwissenschaft. Festschrift für Hajo Bernett.* G. Spitzer and D. Schmitt, eds. Bonn: Institut für Sportwissenschaft und Sport, 1986, pp. 6–74. Translated by A. Krüger. Reproduced with permission.

1. A. Guttmann, *From Ritual to Record—The Nature of Modern Sports* (New York, 1978). German edition: *Vom Ritual zum Rekord—Das Wesen des modernen Sports*, (Schorndorf, 1979).

2. R. D. Mandell, "The Invention of the Sport Record," in: *Stadion* 2 (1976), pp. 250–64; similarly, idem, *Sport—A Cultural History* (New York, 1984), pp. 139–42.

3. For the performances in long-distance running, see St. Oettermann, *Läufer und Vorläufer. Zur Kulturgeschichte des Laufsports* (Frankfurt, 1984).

4. H. Eichberg, "Der Beginn des modernen Leistens," in: *Sportwissenschaft* 4 (1974) pp. 21–48; idem, "Auf Zoll und Quitlein. Sport und Quantifizierungsprozess in der frühen Neuzeit," in: *Archiv für Kulturgeschichte* 56 (1974) pp. 141–76, idem, *Leistung, Spannung, Geschwindigkeit. Sport und Tanz im gesellschaftlichen Wandel des 18./ 19, Jahrhunderts* (Stuttgart, 1978). The author is compiling his results from historical behavior research. His main results, however, are taken from Germany rather than from England.

5. The new quality of physical education as it was reached under the philanthropists was pointed out more than two decades ago by H. Bernett in his monograph *Die Neugestaltung der bürgerlichen Leibesübungen durch die Philanthropen* (Schorndorf, 1960), (1971, 3rd ed.), particularly pp. 88ff. Modern social historians of sport started to do his kind of research only one decade later. A continuation of some of his research with new results can be found in H. Bernett, "Johann Friedrich Christoph GutsMuths," in: *Geschichte der Leibesübungen*, vol. 3, 1, H. Ueberhorst (ed.), (Berlin, 1980), pp. 197–214.

6. A. Krüger and A. Ito, "On the Limitations of Eichberg's and Mandell's Theory of Sports and their Quantification in View of Chikaraishi," in: *Stadion* 3 (1977), pp. 244–52, with answers of Mandell (ibid., p. 257) and Eichberg (ibid., pp. 253–56).

7. Krüger and Ito, "On the Limitations," p. 246, n.9.

8. A review is given by I. Weiler, *Der Sport bei den Völkern der alten Welt* (Darmstadt, 1981), p. 247 (with literature).

9. R. D. Mandell points to the fact in a short note (op. cit., p. 251, note 6) but discards the thought whereas Krüger and Ito take the research of ancient Egypt more seriously (op. cit. p. 246).

10. Weiler, op. cit., p. 144.

11. The Greek traveling author Pausanias, who visited the site in the second century A.D.., describes in great detail (VI, I-XVIII) the forest of victory statutes; see W. W. Hyde, *Olympic Victor Monuments and Greek Athletic Art* (Washington, D.C., 1921); H. V. Hermann, *Olympia. Heiligtum und Wettkampfstätte* (München, 1971), pp. 114.

12. Guttmann recognizes the fact (op. cit. p. 58, Germ. ed.) without drawing the necessary inferences, however.

13. L. Moretti, *I scrizioni agonistiche greche* [Studi pubblicati dall'Istituto Italiano per la storia antica vol. 12], (Rome, 1953), No. 16.

14. J. Ebert, *Griechische Epigramme auf Sieger an gymnischen und hippischen Agonen*

(Abhandlungen der Sächsischen Akademie der Wissenschaften zu Leipzig, Phil.- hist. Kl. vol. 63,2), (Berlin, 1972), p. 107 (with references).

15. Ibid., no. 24.

16. Ibid., no. 22.

17. Die Lieder des Bakchylides. Erster Teil: Die Siegeslieder (H. Maehler, ed.), (Leiden, 1982),1, 160; 4, 6; 10, 13; 11, 7; 14, 8 (referred to by H. V. Herrmann).

18. W. Decker, in: *Stadion* 2 (1976), pp. 107–9.

19. E. Hornung, "Vom Geschichtsbild der alten Ägypter," in: *Geschichte als Fest* (Darmstadt, 1966), pp. 9–29, particularly 15–18.

20. W. Decker, *Die physische Leistung Pharaos. Untersuchungen zu Heldentum, Jagd und Leibesübungen der ägyptischen Könige* (Köln 1971).

21. E. Hornung, "Zur geschichtlichen Rolle des Königs in der 18. Dynastie," in: *Mitteilungen des Deutschen Archäologischen Instituts,* Abt. Kairo 15 (1957), pp. 120–33, quote from p. 125.

22. Ibid., p. 125.

23. E. Hornung, "Zum altägyptischen Geschichtsbewβtsein" (Kölloquium zur allgemeinen und vergleichenden Archäologie vol. 3), (München, 1982), pp. 13–30 (quote from p. 24).

24. This was realized by E. Hornung, "Von zweierlei Grenzen im Alten Ägypten," in: *Eranos-Jahrbuch* 49 (1980), pp. 393–427, 408.

25. E. Hornung, "Politische Planung und Realität im alten Ägypten," in: *Saeculum* 22 (1971), pp. 48–58, 56.

26. E. Hornung, *Tal der Könige,* Zürich, 1983 (2nd ed.), p. 37 (with table on p. 38).

27. Hornung, "Politische Planung," op. cit., p. 57: idem, "Zweierlei Grenzen," op. cit., p. 405.

28. Hornung, "Politische Planung," op. cit., p. 57.

29. Hornung, "Zweierlei Grenzen," op. cit., p. 404.

30. Ibid. One is always reminded of the "agonal principle" which, according to Jacob Burckhardt, was the "motor" of Greek culture. This notion is made more relative by I. Weiler who criticized this "ideology" frequently, first in: *Der Agon im Mythos. Zur Einstellung der Griechen zum Wettkampf* [Impulse der Forschung vol. 16] (Darmstadt, 1974).

31. Hornung, "Zweirlei Grenzen," op. cit., pp. 393–427.

32. M. A. Littauer and J. Crouwel, "Wheeled Vehicles and Ridden Animals in Ancient Near East," in: *Handbuch der Orientalistik,* VII, 1, B-Vorderasien (Leiden, 1979); cf. Chariots and Related Equipment from the Tomb of Tut-'ankhamūn (Tut'ankhamūn's Tomb Series VIII). (Oxford, 1985).

33. An excellent study of this implement comes from W. E. McLeod, *Composite Bows from the Tomb of Tut'ankhamūn* (Tut'ankhamūn Tomb Series III). (Oxford, 1970).

34. G. F. Bass, *Cape Gelidonya. A Bronze Age Shipwreck* (Transactions of the American Philosophical Society, N.S. 57, 8). (Philadelphia, 1967).

35. W. Decker, *Quellentexte zu Sport und Körperkultur im Alten Ägypten* (St. Augustin, 1975) Dokument 14. The stela is from Erment.

36. Ibid., Dok. 19.

37. Ibid., Dok. 20.

38. Ibid., p. 60.

39. E. Edel, "Bemerkungen zu den Schießsporttexten der Könige der 18. Dynastie," in: *Studien zur Altägyptischen Kultur* 7 (1979), pp. 23–39. Cf. particularly pp. 35–38.

40. A fine definition is by K. Weis in: *Sportwissenschaftliches Lexikon,* P. Röthig, ed., (Schorndorf, 1983) (5th ed.), pp. 300.

41. See the references for Table 3.1. On the stela from Erment (Tuthmosis III) it is written: "I am telling you (?) without untruth or lies, what he does in face of the whole army without exaggeration." Cf. Decker, *Quellentexte,* p. 50.

42. Bass, *Cape Gelidonya,* op. cit., p. 52.

43. A composition of the scenes and detailed description are given by J. Vandier, *Manuel d'archéologie égyptienne,* IV (Paris, 1964), pp. 195–216. (cf. VI, Paris, 1978, 336 f., s.v. scribe).

44. Of course, ancient Egypt also had athletic competitions; cf. W. Decker, "Das sogannte Agonale und der altägyptische Sport," M. Görg and E. Pusch, eds., *Festschrift Elmar Edel,* 12 (March 1979) (Studien zu Geschichte, Kultur und Religion Ägyptens und des Alten Testaments, vol. 1), (Bamberg, 1979), pp. 90–104.

45. The only exception from this rule is the above-mentioned inscription from Medamud which is supposed to be from Amenophis II. The pharaoh most likely offered a competition to his officers which never really materialized because of his masterly first attempt; cf. H. Schäfer, "König Amenophis II. als Meisterschütz," in: *Orientalistische Literaturzeitung* 32 (1929), pp. 233–44.

46. Guttmann, *Ritual* (German ed.), p. 59.

47. W. Decker and J. Klauck, "Königliche Bogenschiessleistungen in der 18. ägyptischen Dynastie. Historische Dokumente und Aspekte für eine experimentelle Überprüfung," in: *Kölner Beiträge zur Sportwissenschaft* 3 (1974), pp. 23–55.

48. A last doubt remains as the original copper ingots were not available for obvious reasons.

49. Cf. in particular Hornung, *Geschichte als Fest,* op. cit. (see note 19).

50. Cf. among others A. Hermann, *Die Stelen der thebanischen Felsgräber der 18. Dynastie* (Ägyptologische Forschungen vol. 11), (Glückstadt, 1940), (particularly pp. 128–36).

51. For more literature, see W. Decker, "Art. Leistung, körperliche," *Lexikon der Ägyptologie,* W. Helck and W. Westendorf, eds., vol. III (Wiesbaden, 1980), 100lf.

52. Mandell, *Sport Record,* p. 141, n.2.

4

Recordmania in Sports in Ancient Greece and Rome

DIETRICH RAMBA

Most publications about ancient sports[1] concentrate on the Olympic Games and other pan-Hellenic games. Many detailed analyses have been dedicated to controversial subjects such as the sequence of the disciplines, the winner of the pentathlon or the long jump technique.[2] Even topics like the oiling of athletes,[3] their nudity during competition,[4] their legal status as borrower,[5] or their gluttony[6] have been subject to scholarly analyses.

Since the 1960s B. Bilinski[7] and H. W. Pleket[8] have published a number of works concerning the social history of ancient sports. They refute or correct many commonly accepted views, and they posit the idea that there is not a vast difference between the ancient and modern athlete.

One extremely important aspect of ancient sports that has not been adequately considered is the record of the ancient athlete.[9] Monographs usually broach the topic only briefly, and it is often maintained that the ancients did not care to keep such records.[10] For example, E. N. Gardiner has said that "the Greeks kept no records" and that they "paid more attention to style than to record."[11] Nevertheless, they did use the term *record* for outstanding achievements several times.[12]

Two other aspects of sports records have to be mentioned before we take a more detailed look at the sources. A record is measured not only in centimeters–grams–seconds (c–g–s), but also in terms of national and international successes. Tennis players set records with regard either to their successes in Grand Prix or Grand Slam matches or to a total number of victories in a year or in their entire career. Muhammed Ali holds a remarkable record as the only heavyweight boxer to have gained the world championship twice after losing it. The golfer Harry

Lee Bonner holds a unique world record with 66 holes-in-one. With 707 successes in one year in trotting matches, the German champion Heinz Wewering holds the world record. Many more examples could easily be cited.[13] A particular achievement can be declared to be a national or continental record, an indoor or outdoor record, and so on.

In Greek and Roman antiquity all competitors at major sports events were subject to a set of rules.[14] The organizers of competitions strove to achieve the highest possible standardization, for example, in the drawing of the track[15] and the cleverly designed starting gates for the running competitions[16] and equestrian events.[17] To some extent sports equipment was standardized.[18] A board of supervising referees ensured that every discipline was carried out correctly and according to the rules.[19] The winners, and from time to time official scribes, recorded the winners and their extraordinary achievements.[20]

Before we examine individual records, let us take a look at the description of the victories and the circumstances under which they were achieved. The terms used to characterize these victories as spectacular or that definitely declare them to be records are very revealing. Most of these terms and formulas are found in the inscriptions of ancient victorious athletes, the modern parallel of which is today's sports news.

Achievement and success were finely distinguished for all disciplines. Occasionally athletes proudly pointed out that they had been admitted to certain competitions.[21] It was sometimes noted that somebody had put up a brave fight[22] or had made the final[23]; even a draw could mean fame.[24] A particularly brilliant victory was acknowledged as such,[25] as was also the achievement of a victory without a free draw in the preliminary rounds.[26] An athlete could gain special prestige when his opponents, acknowledging his superiority, did not challenge him at all.[27] Of course, every athlete aspired to undefeated status either in particular contests or in his entire career.[28]

A sign of special superiority was to achieve two or more victories in one day[29] and perhaps in different age groups.[30] An athlete who had been successful in different disciplines was regarded as very versatile.[31] Great attention was given to an athlete who won the same competition year after year or for even more than a decade[32] or at sporting events in which he had participated several times running.[33] In all disciplines carried out at the pan-Hellenic games, the Periodonikēs—a title bestowed on a man who won at all four "crown" festivals[34]—was regarded as especially famous. Greater renown was bestowed on an athlete who won the cycle several times,[35] gained the title of Periodonikēs in different disciplines,[36] or was successful at these four in the shortest possible time.[37]

At the end of the inscriptions of winning athletes, we often find detailed information about their number of victories in "Sacred Games,"[38] in games for prize money,[39] or in events that took place only every four or even two years.[40] Formulas were very common, which meant that it was difficult[41] or even impossible to name all the victories.[42]

Many athletes claimed a record with a formula "one and only."[43] Often, however, the uniqueness and priority of their achievements—for example, a victory, a series,[44] or a combination[45] of successes—were not related to the guild of all athletes but referred only to the athletes of a certain district or merely the native place of the champion.[46]

Let us now turn to record performances in the individual disciplines that surpass those mentioned above, and begin with the combative sport. For a wrestler it was a sign of superiority if he won the fight after only three out of five possible rounds.[47] He was given special praise if he had neither been driven to his knees[48] nor touched the ground with his shoulder.[49] Also brilliant were those wrestlers who had never even been in a critical situation.[50] The famous wrestler T. Claudius Marcianus only had to disrobe to make his opponent give up.[51]

In boxing two champions are well known. Melancomas of Caria remained uninjured in numerous fights and looked like a runner.[52] He could keep his arms in defensive position for two days and, using this technique, wear his opponent down.[53] Theogenes of Tasos achieved better results in the pan-Hellenic games than anyone before him.[54] In the twenty-two years of his career he scored 1,300 victories[55] and never lost a single fight.[56] The pankration (a pugilistic sport combining boxing, wrestling, and street fighting), too, had its champions, above all M. Aurelius Asclepiades. A detailed inscription reports that he never ended a fight in a draw, that he never won by a foul, and that none of his victories was disputed.[57] Athletes who won the pankration, as well as the wrestling in the same Olympic Games, were called "Successor of Heracles." There were only seven of these athletic superstars in antiquity.[58]

Records in running events were numerous. Since stopwatches[59] were unknown, records were set by the number of victories at major sporting events. An athlete who had won three races in one day was given the honorary title "Triastes."[60] Leonidas of Rhodos, given this title four times in Olympia, was praised as the greatest runner in antiquity.[61] The winners of the race in armor at Plataiai were praised as *aristos Hellēnon*. This race was regarded as particularly difficult because of its exceptionally long distance and because the participants were clothed in complete armor.[62] With regard to long-distance running, some records have been handed down to us. Ageos of Argos won the long-distance race at the 133th Olympic Games (328 B.C.) and reported his success on the same day in his hometown more than 100 km away.[63] Drymos of Argos surpassed his fellow countryman when he took part in the opening ceremony of the Olympic Games and reported this event in Epidauros, 140 km from Olympia on the same day.[64] In the Roman Circus an adult who ran the whole day covered a distance of *CLX passuum* (about 237 km).[65]

The more technical disciplines, such as javelin throwing, discus throwing, and the long jump, were less popular and were usually only carried out within the pentathlon. The famous pentathlete Phayllos of Kroton who jumped 55 feet[66] was regarded as world champion in ancient times.[67]

Records were also kept in other sports disciplines. A girl from Sparta, for example, held the record with 1,000 hits in Biasis, a game in which the participants had to kick their back with their heels.[68] In archery a certain Anaxagoras achieved a distance of 282 fathoms (501. 7 m).[69] Two other records are known in weightlifting: "Bybon's Stone" weighing 143.5 kg and the 480 kg rock of Hermodius of Lamsakos,[71] as seen in inscriptions.

Superstars in ball games were P. Aelius who called himself *pilarius omnium eminentissimus* (the most eminent ball player)[72] and Ursus Togatus who surpassed all his predecessors.[73] Gladiators and *bestiarii* documented their preeminent position by stating the number of opponents[74] they beat or the number of beasts they killed.[75]

The desire to be the best athlete in a particular sport reached its peak in the recordmania of the ancient Roman charioteers.[76] Numerous inscriptions are extant that represent charioteers and their sporting careers.[77] Their successes are described at great length, reflecting pride in their achievements. Not surprisingly then, they used every opportunity available to claim a record for themselves.

The inscriptions often state the charioteer's total number of races during his career[78] and, of course, the number of victories achieved.[79] In addition, the *miliarii*, the exclusive club of charioteers who had achieved at least 1,000 victories, was established.[80] In most inscriptions the total number of victories are recorded under different aspects. Four racing teams were known in imperial times,[81] and since most charioteers participated in all of them, victories were divided into different categories according to the chariot racing stable that had sponsored them.[82] They were further classified as victories with a two-, three-, or four-horse-team.[83] Another aspect was the number of horse teams participating in a race, that is, whether it was a single-entry race or two-entry or more race. The greatest attention was given to the *certamina singularum* (definite single-entry).[84] The way a victory was gained was also analyzed. "Final-Sprint" victories were regarded more highly[85] than those leading from start to finish or succeeding by means of clever tactics.[86] Succeeding in exceptional competitions, like the first race after the parade (a *pompa*) or with inexperienced horses (*equorum anagonum*) was a matter of special interest.[87] Some importance was also ascribed to winning prizes. The profit a charioteer earned was in a sense a reflection of his career.[88] Some charioteers never tired of presenting in great detail their victories in races with extraordinary prizes.[89] Even the achievements of the team horses were noted[90]; 100-time victors (*centenarii*) or 200-time victors (*ducenarii*) acquired great fame.[91]

The inscription for the Lusitanian charioteer Diocles[92] shows that he was a true "recordmaniac."[93] It represents the most comprehensive evidence of a Roman charioteer's successes. The list of successes during his twenty four-year sporting career presents him as one of the most famous charioteers of antiquity (*omnium agitatorum eminentissimus*). He is compared with other charioteers whenever it is to his advantage. It is said that he won 134 victories for the "red party" (one of the Byzantine sports factions), 118 of them in *certamina singularum* (single contests) and that he thereby surpassed Thallus who had held the record until then. He is then compared with a charioteer of the "green party" who was the first since the founding of the city to win the special prize of 50,000 sesterces seven times. Diocles won this prize eight times. Moreover, his successes are compared to those of several charioteers combined. Three charioteers of the "green party" (all of them *militarii*—an exclusive group of charioteers who have 1,000 victories) together won the prize eleven times. Diocles surpassed them with his two leading horses Pompeianus and Lucidus.

On another occasion Diocles is also compared with three very famous and celebrated charioteers of different parties. These three charioteers, among them Scorpus who was praised by Martial, scored four times as many victories as Diocles, and between them they managed to win the 50,000 sesterces price twenty-eight times. But Diocles alone pocketed this sum twenty-nine times. Thus, he became the undisputed holder of the record. The many other records he holds are praised time and again, for example, when he beat the "green" charioteer Fortunatus who won the 50,000 sesterces nine times with his horse Tuscus. Diocles won 50,000 sesterces ten times and once even 60,000 sesterces with his horse Pompeianus. Diocles continually proclaimed new records—*novis coactionibus et nunquam ante titulis scriptis Diocles eminet*. For example, one day he started twice with a six-horse team, and both times he pocketed the prize of 60,000 sesterces. He successfully charioted seven yoked horses (*septem equis in se iunctis*) and won races paying 30,000 sesterces each without the aid of a whip (*sine flagello*). Through these unprecedented victories his fame became widespread.

Diocles not only broke the records of former charioteers of his own party as well as of the other parties, but he also set new standards for his time. His contemporary Pontius Epaphroditus was even more successful, but Diocles had more single victories in entry races and more *eripuit* victories (where the contender wins at the last moment after trailing in second place throughout the race). He was also the most successful charioteer with African horses, especially with his superhorse Pompeianus with whom he won 152 victories. He even surpassed Epaphroditus and Musclosus who at that time were champion charioteers with African horses.

We have seen that ancient athletes believed it was important not only to win but also to emphasize that the performance was exceptional and that it surpassed all former achievements. This recordmania is particularly obvious with the ancient sports stars of the Roman Circus.

NOTES

Abbreviations for journals follow those of the *Année Philologigue*, J. Ernst, ed. (Paris: Societe d'Edition Les Belles Lettres, 1988), 15–37. In addition:

CIG = Corpus Inscriptionum Graecarum
CIL = Corpus Inscriptionum Latinarum
IG = Inscriptiones Graecae
ILS = Inscriptiones Latinae Selectae

1. There are a great number of titles, but only the most important can be mentioned here: E. N. Gardiner, *Athletics of the Ancient World,* 2nd ed. (London: Oxford University

Press, 1955); H. A. Harris, *Greek Athletes and Athletics* (London: Hutchinson, 1964); J. Jüthner, *Die athletischen Leibesübungen der Griechen*, 2 vols., F. Brein, ed. (Vienna: Bohlau, 1965–1968); R. Patrucco, *Lo sport nella Grecia antica* (Florence: Olschki, 1972); I. Weiler, *Der Sport bei den Völkern der Alten Welt*, 2nd. ed. (Darmstadt: Wissenschaftliche Buchgesellschaft, 1988).

2. Cf. J. Ebert, *Zum Pentathlon der Antike* (Berlin: Akademie-Verlag, 1963).

3. Ch. Ulf, "Die Einreibung der griechischen Athleten mit Ol," *Stadion* 5 (1979), 220–38.

4. J. A. Arieti, "Nudity in Greek Athletics," *CW* 68 (1975), 431–36 (with most disputable arguments).

5. A. Wacke, "Athleten als Darlehensnehmer nach römischem Recht." *Gymnasium* 86 (1979), 149–64.

6. J. Bazant, "On the Gluttony of Ancient Greek Athletes," *LF* 150 (1982), 129–31.

7. B. Bilinski, *L'agonistica sportiva nella Grecia antica. Aspetti sociale e ispirazioni letterarie* (Rome: Signorelli, 1961); idem, *Agoni ginnici. Componenti artistiche ed intellettuali nell'antica agonistica greca* (Wroclaw: Ossolineum, 1979).

8. H. W. Pleket, "Some Aspects of the History of the Athletic Guilds," *ZPE* 10 (1973), 197–227; idem, "Zur Soziologie des antiken Sports," *MNIR* 36 (1974), 57–87; idem, "Games, Prizes, Athletes and Ideology," *Stadion* 1 (1975), 49–89.

9. Cf. M. N. Tod, "Greek Record-Keeping and Record-breaking," *CQ* 43 (1949), 105–12; A. Guttmann, *From Ritual to Record. The Nature of Modern Sports* (New York: Columbia University Press, 1978), 30–34, 38–40, 45–46, 58–59.

10. For example, E. N. Gardiner, *Greek Athletic Sports and Festivals* (London: Macmillan, 1910), 2; idem, *Athletics,* 140; B. Schröder, *Der Sport im Altertum* (Berlin: Schoetz, 1927), 45; Jüthner, *Leibesübungen,* Vol. 1, 129–30; H. A. Harris, *Sport in Greece and Rome* (Ithaca, N.Y.: Cornell University Press, 1972), 37.

11. Gardiner, *Athletics,* 140.

12. Ibid., 106, 110, 112ff.

13. Cf. A. Russell, ed., *Guinness Book of Records* (London: Guinness, 1988).

14. Jul. Afric. Ol. 23; Paus. 3,14,10; 8, 40, 3; Philostr. gymn. 12; Hdt. 8, 59; as to the combative sports, cf. W. Rudolph, *Olympischer Kampfsport in der Antike. Faustkampf, Ringkampf und Pankration in den griechischen Nationalfestspielen* (Berlin: Akademie-Verlag, 1965), 11–12, 37–38; 65–66.

15. Paus. 6,1, 2; Lukian. Hermot. 40.

16. O. Broneer, "Excavations of Isthmia. Third Campaign. 1955–6." *Hesperia* 27 (1958), 10–15; idem, "Starting Devices in Greek Stadia," *AJA* 76 (1972), 205–6.

17. H. A. Harris, "The Starting Gate for Chariots at Olympia," *G&R* (1968), 113–26; J. H. Humphrey, *Roman Circuses* (London: Butler and Tanner, 1986), 132–74.

18. Paus. 5,12,8.

19. Paus. 5,9,5; 6,3,7; cf. the numerous paintings of referees on vases.

20. M. I. Finley and H. W. Pleket, *The Olympic Games. The First Thousand Years.* (London: Chatto and Windus, 1976), 132: " . . . we can also assume that the inscriptions in honour of successful athletes and the 'epinikia' of Pindar and Bacchylides contain accurate information."

21. CIG 4241; cf. L. Robert, "Etudes d'épigraphie grecque," *RPh* 4 (1930), 28–29.

22. Cf. L. Robert, "Inscription agonistique d'Ancyre concours d'Ancyre," *Hellenica*

11–12 (1960), 357; idem, *Les épigrammes satiriques de Lucillius sur les athlètes. Parodie et réalités* (Gent: Fondation Hardt, 1968), 186–87.

23. Robert, "Etudes," 28–29; idem, "Epitaphe d'un comedién a Messine," *Hellenica* 11–12 (1960), 334.

24. Cf. J. Ebert, *Griechische Epigramme auf Sieger an gymnischen und hippischen Agonen* (Berlin: Akademie-Verlag, 1972), 229.

25. CIG 3503; cf. L. Robert, "Inscription agonistique d'Ancyre concours d'Ancyre," *Hellenica* 11–12 (1960), 351–52.

26. Cf. L. Moretti, *Iscrizioni agonistiche greche* (Rome: Signorelli, 1953), 171–73.

27. Paus. 6,11,4; Jul. Afric. 01. 118; Plin. n. h. 35, 139; cf. J. Jüthner, "Akoniton-akoniti." *Glotta* 29 (1941), 73–77.

28. Cf. R. Knab, *Die Periodoniken. Ein Beitrag zur Geschichte der gymnischen Agone an den 4 griechischen Hauptfesten* (Giessen: Postberg, 1934), 12.

29. Moretti, *Iscrizioni*, 198–206; Ebert, *Epigramme*, 142–45; cf. R. Merkelbach, "Uber ein ephesisches Dekret für einen Athleten aus Aphrodisias und über Athletentitel paradoxos," *ZPE* 14 (1974), 91–96.

30. Cf. Knab, *Periodoniken*, 37, 65.

31. Paus. 6,11,5; 6,14,2f; Moretti, *Iscrizioni*, 51–56; Ebert, *Epigramme*, 118–26.

32. Knab, *Periodoniken*, 36; Moretti, *Iscrizioni*, 60–62.

33. L. Robert, "Un athlète Milésien," *Hellenica* 7 (1949), 117–25.

34. Cf. Knab, *Periodoniken*, 4–10; L. Moretti, "Note sugli antichi Periodonikai," *Athenaeum* N.S. 32 (1954), 115–20.

35. Cf. Knab, *Periodoniken*, 50–55 (Milon, Glaukos, Theogenes, Dromeus).

36. Jul. Afric. Ol. 178; Aelian. var. hist. 4,15.

37. Cf. Knab, *Periodoniken*, 9.

38. Cf. Moretti, *Iscrizioni*, 244–49; Ebert, *Epigramme*, 250.

39. IG 14m 739; cf. Moretti, *Iscrizioni*, 224–26.

40. CIG 2682; IG 14, 746; Moretti, *Iscrizioni*, 181–86; Harris, *Greek Athletes*, 75.

41. Anth. Pal. 13,14; Ebert, *Epigramme*, 66–69.

42. L. Robert, "Sur les inscriptions de Chios. 3. Inscription agonistique," BCH 57 (1933), 539–43; Ebert, *Epigramme*, 238–45.

43. Cf. Tod, "Greek Record-keeping." 106–8.

44. L. Robert, *Hellenica* 7 (1949), 117–25.

45. Cf. Moretti, *Iscrizioni*, 68–75; Ebert, *Epigramme*, 138–42.

46. IG 12, 1, 841; W. Peek, "Zwei agonistische Gedichte aus Rhodos," *Hermes* 77 (1942), 206–11; Moretti, *Iscrizioni*, 123–25; Ebert, *Epigramme*, 172–75.

47. Philostr. gymn. 11; Anth. Pal. 5,588; Sen. de benef. 5,3.

48. Anth. Pal. 16,24; cf. Robert, *Lucillius*, 252; Patrucco, *Sport*, 302.

49. IG 14, 1107; Anth. Pal. 9,588; 16, 25; Ebert, *Epigramme*, 198–200.

50. Jul. Afric. 01. 98; cf. Knab, *Periodoniken*, 14; R. Merkelbach, "Der griechische Wortschatz und die Christen," *ZPE* 18 (1975), 146–48; M. Poliakoff, *Studies in the Terminology of Greek Combat Sports* (Cologne: Hain, 1982), 42–44.

51. W. Crönert, "Delphische Weihepigramme," *JOEAI* 12 (1909), 151–53; L. Robert, "Inscription agonistique de Smyrne," *Hellenica* 7 (1949), 110.

52. Dion. Chrys. 28,7.

53. Dion. Chrys. 27,11; cf. Finley/Pleket, *Games*, 84–85.

54. W. Peek, "Delphische Gedichte," *MDAI* (A) 67 (1942), 232–69; Moretti, *Iscrizioni*, 51–56; Ebert, *Epigramme*, 118–26.

55. Pausanias 6,11,5 mentions about 1,400 victories; Plutarch praec. publ. ger. 15,7 counts 1,200.

56. Cf. D. C. Young, *The Olympic Myth of Greek Amateur Athletics* (Chicago: Ares, 1984), 96–97.

57. IG 14, 1102; Gardiner, *Athletes*, 112 (with some false interpretations); Moretti, *Iscrizioni*, 228–35.

58. Cf. Knab, *Periodoniken*, 6.

59. H. A. Harris, "Stadia and Starting Grooves," *G&R* 7 (1960), 28; "The Greeks were mercifully free from the tyranny of the stop-watch."

60. Jul. Afric. 01. 67; Philostr. gymn. 33; cf. Moretti, *Iscrizioni*, 155; Ebert, *Pentathlon*, 5; Patrucco, *Sport*, 124; Finley/Pleket, *Games*, 122.

61. Paus. 6,13,4; cf. F. Mezo, *Geschichte der Olympischen Spiele* (Munich: Knorr and Hirth, 1930), 73.

62. Philostr. gymn. 8; Paus. 9,2,6; cf. L. Robert, "Recherches epigraphiques," *REA* 31 (1929), 13–20; Knab, *Periodoniken*, 14; Moretti, *Iscrizioni*, 119.

63. Jul. Afric. 01. 113; cf. Mezo, *Geschichte*, 77.

64. IG 4,1349; cf. H. Bengtson, "Aus der Lebensgeschichte eines griechischen Distanzläufers," *SO* 32 81956, 38–39.

65. Plin. n. h. 7, 84; cf. J. Suolakti, "The Origin of the Story about the First Marathonrunner," *Arctos* 5 (1967), 131; V. J. Matthews, "The Hemerodromei. Ultra Long-distance Running in Antiquity," *CW* 68 (1974), 167–68.

66. Cf. Moretti, *Iscrizioni*, 27; Ebert, *Pentathlon*, 35; Patrucco, *Sport*, 70.

67. Poll. 3,151; Eustath. comm. ad hom. Od. 8,1591; Zenob 6,23.

68. Poll. 4,102.

69. E. v. Stern, "Der Pfeilschuss des Olbiopoliten Anaxagoras," *JOEAI* 4 (1901), 57–60; W. McLeod, "The Range of the Ancient Bow," *Phoenix* 19 (1965), 6.

70. J. Zingerle, "Der Steinwurf des Bybon," *Commentationes Vindobonenses* 2 (1936), 111–12; Moretti, *Iscrizioni*, 4–6.

71. IG 12, 3, 449; cf. R. Herzog, "Die Wunderheilung von Epidaurus," Philologus Suppl. 22 (1931), 110–17.

72. CIL 6, 8997; cf. S. Mendner, *Das Ballspiel im Leben der Völker* (Münster: Aschendorff, 1956), 83.

73. CIL 6, 9797; ILS 5173; cf. Mendner, *Ballspiel*, 84.

74. L. Robert, *Les gladiateurs dans l'Orient grèc* (Paris: H. Champion, 1940), 113–115; 166–67; 199–200.

75. Robert, *Gladiateurs*, 107, 130.

76. For records of charioteers in the Byzantine hippodrome, see A. Cameron, *Porphyrius the Charioteer* (Oxford: Clarendon Press, 1973), 206–14.

77. Cf. L. Friedländer, *Roman Life and Manner Under the Early Empire*. 4 vols. (London: Routledge, 1908–1913), vol. 2, 24.29; J.P.V.D. Balsdon, *Life and Leisure in Ancient Rome* (New York: McGraw-Hill, 1969), 314–24.

78. CIL 6, 10047; 10050; ILS 5285; 5287.

79. CIL 6, 10048; 10063; ILS 5281; 5285.

80. Cf. Friedländer, *Roman Life*, Vol. 4, 180; R. Palmieri, "Ricordi di ludi circenses a Teanum Sidicinum," *RAAN* 53 (1978), 60; Weiler, *Sport*, 246.

81. Cf. Friedländer, *Roman Life*, Vol. 2, 37–38; A. Cameron, *Circus Factions. Blues and Greens at Rome and Byzantium* (Oxford: Clarendon Press, 1976), 5–23.

82. CIL 6, 10047; 10063; ILS 5281; 5286.

83. Two-horse teams were driven primarily by beginners, whereas the stars of the circus sometimes drove 6-, 7-, 8-, and 10-horse teams; cf. Balsdon, *Life*, 316.

84. Cf. Friedländer, *Roman Life*, Vol. 4, 181. H. A. Harris, *Sport in Greece and Rome* (Ithaca, N.Y.: Cornell University Press, 1972), 198.

85. CIL 6, 10048 also states which party had been defeated in a final dash.

86. Cf. Friedländer, *Roman Life*, Vol. 4, 191; Harris, *Sport*, 199–200.

87. CIL 6, 10047; ILS 5288.

88. CIL 6, 10048; 10050; ILS 5286; 5288.

89. CIL 6, 10047; 10049; ILS 5286; 5288.

90. CIL 6, 10053.

91. Cf. Friedländer, *Roman Life*, Vol. 4, 192.

92. CIL 6, 10048; ILS 5287; cf. N. Lewis and M. Reinhold, *Roman Civilization. Selected Readings II: The Empire* (New York: Columbia University Press, 1955), 230–31; Garcia y Bellido, "El Espanol C. Apuleius Diocles El Mas Famoso Corredor De Carros De La Antiquëdad," *Citius, Altius, Fortius 14* (1972), 5–17.

93. Martial 10, 53; 11, 1.

5

Sports Records In Medieval England: An Inquiry

JOHN MARSHALL CARTER

According to the historian Suetonius, Julius Caesar saw a statue of Alexander the Great at Cadiz and lamented that he (Caesar) had accomplished nothing compared to the Macedonian *Wunderkind*. Of course, Caesar was not the only great man to aspire to the kind of greatness that Alexander attained. Throughout late antiquity and the Middle Ages, would-be Alexanders tortured themselves trying to equal the record of the Macedonian who built one of history's great empires. Although the empire itself had crumbled shortly after the death of Alexander, the abstract of such a feat remained fresh in the minds of historians and public men alike.[1]

Good books make us think. They may not change our minds, but they often encourage us to reevaluate our ideas. The famous British historian A. J. P. Taylor, for one, has written several books that have made us take another look at the First and Second World Wars. His *Origins of the Second World War* comes to mind immediately. Indeed, historiography benefits from conceptualizers who force us into reassessing our previous positions on historical problems.[2]

Allen Guttmann's *From Ritual to Record: The Nature of Modern Sports* (1978), has mandated that we review our beliefs about the origins and development of modern sports.[3] Widely praised for its originality and verve, *From Ritual to Record* has become one of the most important publications in the rapidly expanding field of sports history.[4] The book is not without its critics, for that, too, is part of the weight good books must bear.[5] Several areas of sports which Guttmann examines in the book have been criticized by sports historians in America, Europe, and Japan.[6] One area in particular, sports records, has generated some interesting debate. On page 54 of *From Ritual to Record* Guttmann has set up a table that presents characteristics of sports in various ages.[7] In this table, Guttmann concludes that there were no precursors of modern sports records in primitive times, in ancient Greece and Rome, and in medieval Europe. Leaving the first three historical periods to scholars in these fields (see Chapters 3 and 4 in this volume), we will investigate the possibility of sports records in medieval England.[8]

Guttmann asked: "What is a record in our modern sense? It is the marvelous abstraction that permits competition not only among those gathered together on the field of sport but also among them and others distant in time and space."[9] Did marvelous abstractions of sports exist in medieval England? In attempting what will be at least partial answers to this question, we will try to broaden the scope of the debate over the origins of sports records. In Chapter 7, Joachim Rühl will also address a related area of sports in preindustrial societies. He will specifically examine the scoring at tournaments in Tudor and Stuart England.

In order to investigate the possibility of sports records in medieval England, it is important first to establish some chronological and cultural parameters. Of prime importance is the chronology of records that reveal facets of life in medieval England. Was there a crucial period in the English Middle Ages when records— in the modern sense—began to establish a basis for relying on the printed word against the shortcomings of memory?[10] According to M. T. Clanchy in his thought-provoking book entitled *From Memory to Written Record* (1979), the Norman Conquest of England accelerated the necessity of records because of the near revolution in land tenure: the Norman aristocracy became the great landowning class of England.[11] When William the Conqueror finally became interested in his newly conquered realm, he set about to record its length and breadth, its farmland and its potential, in one of the most important economic records of all time, the *Domesday Book*.[12]

Between the *Domesday Book* (1086) and Edward I's great survey *quo warranto* in 1290, medieval England was transformed into a society of written record.[13] Although the previous centuries had known records of various types, the twelvth and thirteenth centuries witnessed a veritable record explosion in England.[14] The High Middle Ages in England (which for this chapter is ca. 1066–1300) witnessed a geometric increase in the quantity and quality of records about nearly every aspect of society.[15] Medieval English kings and their increasingly complex bureaucracies sought to quantify important areas of life. One collection of thirteenth-century charters, for example, the *Registrum Antiquissimum* of Lincoln Cathedral, contains 2,890 records in the printed edition. In only one session of the royal court in an eyre in an average-sized county during the reign of Edward I, over 2,000 documents could be produced.[16]

Anglo-Norman and Angevin society had grown more complex than, say, the age of Alfred the Great (871–899). In 1194, the year King Richard I licensed the tournament, England was in the wake of its record explosion. Added to bureaucratic complexities was the fact that a French-speaking nobility had imposed its law and customs on a new land. Multilingualism and multilegalism demanded more than the power of memory and the administrative machinery of Anglo-Saxon England (although the Normans preserved many of the Anglo-Saxons' legal ideas, such as the writ). Life had grown more complex, however. In the legal sphere, for example, the thirteenth century witnessed a tremendous division of labor among the royal bureaucracy. Because the king could not be everywhere at once, the king's royal justices and administrators took royal authority into the corners of the realm. Their business was so great that only written records could help them remember it all. Indeed, the amount of extant legal records from the thirteenth century is almost staggering in its volume and complexity. When we add criminal matters to tenurial, military, financial, political, religious, and recreational matters, the age of records (1066–1300) becomes much clearer.[17]

Even though the above examples constitute evidence for a record-oriented society on the verge of flowering, these records are not the "marvelous abstractions" that Guttmann pointed to in *From Ritual to Record*. They are abstracts, but they do not have the living quality of the sports record. However, like the sports record, these records reflect the workings of a society concerned with its ever-present past. A feel for the past is not a product of modern society.

Even though there were records of varying size and complexity, were there "marvelous abstractions" of sports and recreations? We have established a basis for a record-oriented society (not sports records at this juncture of the chapter, but records providing evidence of a maturing—if not completely mature—sophisticated civilization directly in touch with its past and keenly alive to the importance of print media). Although outside the boundaries of this chapter, it might be added here that M. T. Clanchy's thesis pushes back the origins of the "Gutenberg Galaxy" into the twelfth century (before Gutenberg). Indeed, to go another step, we might argue that the zeal to quantify expressed by thirteenth-century English bureaucrats, both lay and ecclesiastical, foreshadows the quantifying zealots of the Newtonian Age. To illustrate the last comment, we might ask, how can an eighteenth-century (modern?) government know more about its constituencies than William the Conqueror's Domesday inquisitors knew about late eleventh-century England? The simple answer is that they could not.

A judicious selection of records from the period under investigation should prove useful in trying to uncover sports records in medieval England. In *From Memory to Written Record,* Clanchy organizes medieval English records (ca. 1066–ca. 1300) into the following categories: charters; chirographs (which recorded two-party agreements); certificates; letters; writs (brief, executive orders); memoranda kept by institutions (such as financial accounts, surveys, and rentals); legal records; year books (reports of court cases); chronicles; cartularies; registers; learned works (such as *summae*), and literary works (such as *chansons de gestes*).[18] Many of the categories can be divided into several subcategories. Legal records, for example, included eyre rolls, assize rolls, records of sessions of oyer and terminer, and trailbaston records. Clanchy presents some impressive figures about the great quantities of documents: "Eight million charters may have been written in the thirteenth century alone for smallholders and serfs." In addition to staggering numbers of documents, various literate modes were spread throughout every village and bailiff in England in the thirteenth century. In this age, written records supported memory in a substantial way.[19]

SPORTS RECORDS IN MEDIEVAL ENGLAND

Did the record explosion in England in the High Middle Ages include sports records as we know them today? In answering this important question, it is necessary to establish why sports records would have existed and so the act of defining sports becomes important. For this chapter, sports are defined as the activities people engaged in for entertainment, diversion, and pastime.[20] Although the medieval tournament (which has become increasingly well known to students of sports history because of important recent studies) conforms more readily to the recent rigid definitions of sports, this study is not necessarily limited to the tournament. However, because an overwhelming number of primary sources are concerned with the tournament and other sports of the nobility such as hunting and hawking, this chapter will reflect such an imbalance.[21]

The tournament in all of its multiplicity of forms (melee, joust, feat of arms, etc.), hunting, and hawking were sports requiring not only a great deal of skill by the sports persons involved in them, but also expensive equipment. Recently, Juliet R. V. Barker has shown that tournaments from the twelfth to the fifteenth centuries increased in expense and that rising costs created a smaller and smaller group of tourneyers. Tourneying in particular touched nearly all spheres of royal and noble life: political, military, economic, religious, and social. It is only logical to assume that the kings, the church, and the feudal aristocracy would be interested in such a wide-ranging phenomenon.[22] And, as has been stated above, important matters in England (and elsewhere) in the High Middle Ages were recorded for posterity. Sports, such as tourneying, hunting, and hawking, were very important and, subsequently, were made a part of the growing number of written records.[23] A few illustrations should help underscore the importance of records, but the records should also demonstrate the growing importance of sports: so important that sports events, persons, and feats were recorded for posterity.

For example, Jean Froissart, in his *Chronicles of England and France,* related that "During the time in which these things were passing, the three knights . . . Sir Boucicant the Younger, the lord Reginald de Roye and the lord de Saimpi, were making preparations to fulfill their engagement. This tournament had been proclaimed in many countries, but especially in England."[24]

Froissart also illustrates techniques used in the fourteenth century: "When the two knights had for a short time eyed each other, they spurred their horses and met full gallop with such force, that Sir Boucicant pierced the shield of the earl of Huntingdon, and the point of his lance slipped along his arm, but without wounding him.''[25]

The herald of Sir John Chandos reiterates the pageantry of tournaments in his *Life of the Black Prince:*

> Great joy and great feast were made, and great
> joustings cried then through the country.[26]

Chronicles, like those of Froissart and the herald of Sir John Chandos, were natural narratives for the exploits of the knightly class. However, nonliterary records should also be considered in any investigation of sports and pastimes in medieval England. The liberate rolls (containing information about crown expenditures) of King Henry III (1216–1272) bristle with sports-oriented orders. A royal directive of July 16, 1252, states:

To the sheriff of Northampton: *Contrabreve* to find necessaries for six falcons of the king's and four of Edward the king's son which are in the keeping of Ralph of Erlham, and three greyhounds of the king's and two of Edward's, that is, a halfpenny daily for each falcon and each greyhound, and one and one-half pence daily for livery of a groom keeping them, from the time when the sheriff first received the county as long as the falcons are in moult.[27]

Even legal records contain valuable information for the sports historian. Furthermore, the information from legal and other records of the High Middle Ages in England is very detailed . It is not unusual to find sports-related criminal acts recorded in the eyre and coroners' rolls. The legal scribes recorded in the London eyre of 1276 that "Richard de Borham with many other people from London went to a wrestling match at Bermundseye outside of the city and there wrestled with the men of the prior of Bermundseye."[28]

Minstrels and *jongleurs* sang of the adventures of both fictional and factual tournament professionals. The Provençal troubadour Bertran de Born wrote with an unbridled glee about the pageantry of war and tournaments (and the heroes of both):

The gay time of Easter pleases me, bringing leaves and flowers, and I am pleased when I hear the sounds of birds making their song ring throughout the woodland, and I love to see the fields pitched with tents and pavilions and I'm happy to see in ranks in the countryside armed knights and horses . . .

When the fight starts we shall see war-clubs, swords, colored helmets, shields, sliced, ruined, and many a liegeman strike in the melee, so that dead men's horses and those of the dying will wander aimlessly.

When he's in the thick of it let no man of birth think of anything but splitting heads and arms, for a dead man is worth more than a live prisoner.[29]

Manuscript illuminations, psalters, and tapestries also chronicled the exploits of both real and imaginary heroes. Interestingly, Provençal songbooks were illustrated with troubadours dressed in the accoutrements of knights. Bertran de Born is pictured in knight's armor and riding a charger in the Provençal "M" songbook.[30] L. Kendrick believes that the illustration underscores the daring-do of Bertran's lyrics. However, it seems possible that the troubadour may have wanted to be dressed like one of his knightly subjects in his verse. At any rate, the troubadour lyrics provide us with another record of sporting events and sportsmen.

Added to the "records" mentioned above can be tourneying retinues, like the two for the Dunstable tournaments of 1309 and 1334, which preserve the names and identities of literally thousands of tournament-goers. Records such as the *Roll of Purchase Made for the Tournament of Windsor Park (1278)* provide fine details on equipment for tournaments, and provisions for tourneyers and spectators.[31]

The challenges issued by jousters to potential competitors and the conversations of jousters have been preserved in chronicles.[32] Admittedly, the great majority of them may have been created by the chronicler and put into the mouths of the warriors. Writers like Bertran de Born and Jean Froissart, however, were intimates of great warriors and certainly understood the warrior's milieu. For example, Froissart recorded a conversation among knights as they traveled together in which one knight compared the fighting abilities of the Armagnacs and the Foixiens. When traveling, at tournaments or in great halls, knights talked about their favorite subjects: tourneying, hunting, hawking, and making war.[33] Knightly conversations generally included discussion of the abilities of other knights.[34] On the same journey mentioned above, the chronicler Froissart mentioned that his traveling companion described another knight, Garses du Chatel, as "a very valiant knight."[35]

Royal and noble wardrobe account books contain valuable information about tourneying and other forms of royal and noble sport. Close, patent, and liberate rolls also constitute valuable records of sports in England from ca. 1150 to ca. 1400. Preachers often mentioned jousts, jousters, or other sports in their sermons.[36] Bernard of Clairvaux, who had been a knight himself before becoming a Cistercian monk, maintained his chivalric vocabulary even in his sermons and other writings. His "Office of St. Victor" is especially noteworthy for the martial/ludic-metaphoric language that is recorded:

> O victorious soul . . . like a sparrow,
> avoided the fowler's snare . . .
> O veteran soldier . . .
> we though are still engaged
> amid hostile swords . . .
> O Victor renowned, how gloriously
> you triumphed over the foe . . .

O victorious Jesus, yours was the victory
O Victor indeed! As long as you
lived, you lifted the banner
of victory in triumph
Your victories give us heart;
may your weaponry give us security.[37]

Papal prohibitions of tournaments, such as those recorded in the proceedings of the Council of Clermont of 1130, are records of sport (of a sort), even though they are negative in their assessment of sport.[38] Then, of course, there is the fictional literature: poems (although many poems were also written about real-life warriors), *chansons* (again, real-life characters were included), and ballads. Although the fictive image of the medieval sportsperson is beyond the scope of this chapter, it should be said that fictional or semifictional characters such as Arthur, Lancelot, Roland, and Siegfried had a profound impact on real-life sportsmen.[39] Indeed, the fictive element may even have helped to forge the mental image for society of the real-life sportsman. The herald of Sir John Chandos wrote about King Edward III that he was "of such noble disposition, for God had given him such virtue that since the time of King Arthur there was no king of such power."[40] "Sir Gawain was a fictive hero who was "of bewte' and debonerte' and blythe semblaunt.""[41]

In this age of records, it is interesting to speculate about the continuity of the heroic reputation and what constitutes that reputation. Gervase Matthew has suggested the basic continuity of the heroic reputation of William the Marshal (ca. 1149–1219) in the person of Edward the Black Prince (1330–1376).[42] In this period (the eleventh through fourteenth centuries) was there developing a factual heroic image that paralleled the fictive heroic image? It is very probable. Who or what perpetuated the heroic image of medieval sportsmen such as William the Marshal or Edward the Black Prince? In addition to the above records that have been delineated, we should also add the important service of the heralds (who may also provide us with a clue about reputation-building and reputation continuity). Their function at medieval tournaments is of extreme importance in a discussion of sports records in England in the Middle Ages. N. Denholm-Young has said that after Richard I sanctioned the tournament in England in 1194, the function of heralds crystallized: "[Heralds] . . . travelled through the countryside and even abroad to proclaim a forthcoming event, made the arrangements, announced the competitors, kept the score, declared the victors, and marshalled the processions to and from the list."[43]

More recently, scholars in England and West Germany have discussed the role of heralds in medieval tournaments. Juliet Barker demonstrates that the heralds were also responsible "for producing the elaborate formal jousting challenges of the late fourteenth century."[44] Joachim Rühl, concludes that it was the heralds who determined the best jouster by adding up the scores. In an assertion that differs markedly from Barker, Rühl shows that heralds, and not women, awarded prizes to the winners of tournaments.[45] Georges Duby's recent biography of the famous knight William Marshal probably contains the best delineation of the twelfth-and thirteenth-century herald's functions. Duby, basing his refreshing short biography of the Marshal on the thirteenth-century life of the Earl Marshal entitled *Histoire de Guillaume le Maréchal,* writes:

> The advertising function [of tournaments] was performed, we may suppose, by those known as heralds, professionals in identifying and extolling the participants, capable of recognizing all the knights . . . by the heraldic signs they displayed, expert too in the art of composing and interpreting a refrain to launch this team or that champion, lauding their feats and, for a share of the profits, advancing their worth.[46]

Therefore, heralds played a vital role in creating and sustaining reputations for tourneyers. We turn now to the life of the man who may have had the greatest reputation as a medieval tournament professional, William the Marshal.

THE RECORD AND THE RECORD-MAKER

Baseball enthusiasts in modern America would not think of separating the sportsman from the sports record. The fact that sixty homeruns in one season became that "marvelous abstraction" from 1927 until 1961 did not mean that Babe Ruth was left out of the picture. Newspapers, biographies, baseball cards, television and radio programs, movies, speeches, sermons, the Baseball Hall of Fame's oral and written information media, trophies, the discussion of Little Leaguers as they talked of their heroes do not separate the record and the record-maker. Indeed, any mention of the sports record almost always brings to mind the record-maker. Although it is speculation, it seems fairly reasonable to assume that generations of would-be record-makers would not separate the sixty homeruns from the "Sultan of Swat." When Roger Maris hit sixty-one homers in 1961, he was not only breaking the record for homeruns, but he was breaking *Ruth's* record. This kind of reasoning seems quite appropriate for sports and potential sports records in medieval England.

The great medieval sportsman William the Marshal found a type of immortality in one of the most important of all biographical records from the Middle Ages. William the Marshal, an English knight and the earl of Pembroke, is one of the best examples of medieval social mobility. A younger son of a relatively middling knight, the Marshal climbed the ranks of knighthood and fame with his prowess in the tournament. When he died in 1219, he was honored in much of north-western Europe as the greatest knight who ever lived. Indeed, to receive such accolades, the Marshal almost takes his place alongside the great fictive knights of twelfth- and thirteenth-century literature. William Marshal became, in a sense, a real-life Gawain or Galahad.

It is believed that his trusted esquire, John of Earley, provided much of the detail for the *History of William the Marshal* that was commissioned by William

Marshal's eldest son and written between 1225 and 1226 by a poet known only as John. The *History* is considered to be an accurate picture of William Marshal and of Anglo-French chivalry in the twelfth and thirteenth centuries. When John the Poet recounts the years 1173–1183, a period he encapsulates into over 2,500 lines of the *History,* tournaments dominate the narrative. As Georges Duby has noted, probably no other record from the Middle Ages gives us a better account of tournaments. Duby's translation of the *History* allows modern readers to understand the excitement of the twelfth and thirteenth-century tournament.[47]

The prizes awarded, the numbers of knights and booty captured, the feats of daring-do never before seen, and other exploits helped to form the public image of famous sportsmen like William the Marshal. Although feats like the Marshal's rescue of the Young King (Henry II's oldest son) in a tournament further enhanced his glittering reputation, they do not conform to what Guttmann meant by ''marvelous abstractions.'' Do we find marvelous abstractions in *The History of William the Marshal*? The answer is yes.

The passage contained in lines 18481–96 includes the following statement by William the Marshal himself: ''I have taken five hundred knights with their arms, horses and entire equipment.''[48] As in the attempts to emulate the Marshal's loyalty, bravery, and prowess, so must many of the tourneyers who lived long after the Marshal have sought to reach the Marshal's record of 500 knights captured. As Georges Duby relates, ''Another memorial had to be built, a secular one capable of circulating the dead man's renown within the social space in which he had been illustrious.''[49] Duby goes on to explain that the biography was composed to be read publicly by a reader so that the great tourneyer's life, and his record of 500 knights captured, could be celebrated in the encampments built beside the tournament grounds.[50] Future generations, like William the Marshal's own son Gilbert who was killed in a tournament in Hertford in 1241, must surely have sought to break the great tourneyer's record.[15]

Although William the Marshal is perhaps the best example of the medieval tournament professional, he was, of course, not alone. Fulk Fitz Warin, the Chatelain de Couci, Marshal Boucicaut, Ulrich von Lichenstein, and Richard Beauchamp, to name a few, were great tourneyers whose exploits are preserved for posterity in written records.

CONCLUSIONS

The period from 1066 through 1300 in England witnessed a veritable record explosion. Almost every sphere of life became a matter of written records. Sports, particularly royal and noble sports such as tourneying, hawking, and hunting, involved considerable expense, reflected the world-view of the powerful, and touched nearly every other sphere of life. Yet, recording the cost of a charger used in a tournament or even listing the names of participants in a tournament does not constitute what Guttmann meant by sports records in the modern sense (''marvelous abstractions''), where a record is set by a sportsman and sportsmen in subseqent ages can pursue the record long after the record-maker is dead. But in the case of William the Marshal's record of capturing 500 knights in tournaments in the twelfth and thirteenth centuries, recorded in *The History of William the Marshal* and then read and re-read by a professional reader to tourneyers long after the Marshal's death, we have what appears to be a sports record in the modern sense. In light of this evidence, it is apparent that the debate over the origins of sports records needs expansion. It is possible that the search for the origins of modern sports records in premodern societies may be the incorrect approach. At this juncture, the more plausible approach to the problem might be to look for the evidence of the medieval sports record in the modern world.

NOTES

1. Suetonius, *The Twelve Caesars*, trans. by Robert Graves (Harmondsworth, 1957), p. 12.

2. A.J.P. Taylor, *The Origins of the Second World War* (New York, 1961).

3. Allen Guttmann, *From Ritual to Record: The Nature of Modern Sports* (New York, 1978).

4. Cf. the reviews of *From Ritual to Record* in the 1978 and 1979 numbers of the *Journal of Sport History*.

5. The earliest criticism of the thesis put forward by Henning Eichberg and Richard Mandell was Arnd Krüger and Akira Ito's "On the Limitations of Eichberg's and Mandell's Theory of Sports and Their Quantification in View of Chikaraishi," *Stadion* 3, 2 (1977) pp. 244–56. This article has been reprinted as a chapter in the present book.

6. Ibid.

7. *From Ritual to Record*, p. 54.

8. However, many of the sportsmen whose lives will be observed in this chapter had reputations known on the continent as well as in England.

9. *From Ritual to Record*, p. 54.

10. Dorothy Whitelock, *The Audience of Beowulf* (Oxford, 1951).

11. M. T. Clanchy, *From Memory to Written Record* (Oxford, 1979), pp. 1–20.

12. Numerous scholars have written eloquently about the significance of this important economic document from the late eleventh century. The nine hundredth anniversary of the compilation in 1986 witnessed a new wave of interest.

13. Clanchy, *From Memory to Written Record*, p. 8.

14. Ibid.

15. These records have formed the bases of numerous social, legal, and economic studies.

16. Ibid., pp. 8–9.

17. C.A.F. Meekings, *Studies in Thirteenth Century Justice and Administration* (London, 1981).

18. Clanchy, *From Memory to Written Record*, pp. 10–22.

19. Ibid.

20. For too long in the short history of sports studies, research has been thwarted by narrow squabbles over definition.

21. Juliet R. V. Barker, *The Tournament in England, 1100–1400* (Woodbridge, Suffolk, 1986) presents a diverse number of records in this important study.

22. Ibid.

23. See, for example, Friedrich II, *The Art of Falconry*, trans. and ed. C. A. Wood and F. M. Fyfe (London, 1943).

24. Jean Froissart, *Chronicles*, trans. Thomas Johnes (New York, 1860), p. 509.

25. Ibid.

26. Herald of Sir John Chandos, *Life of the Black Prince*, (London, 1956), p. 139.

27. *Calendar of Liberate Rolls* IV, p. 61.

28. Martin Weinbaum, *The London Eyre of 1276* (London, 1976), case 116.

29. Quoted in L. Kendrick, *The Game of Love: Troubadour Wordplay* (Berkeley, 1987).

30. Ibid., p. 110.

31. *Roll of Purchases Made for the Tournament of Windsor Park* (1278).

32. N. Denholm-Young, "The Tournament in the Thirteenth Century," p. 255.

33. Froissart, *Chronicles*, p. 364.

34. Ibid.

35. Ibid.

36. See the valuable study by G. R. Owst, *Literature and Pulpit in Medieval England* (Oxford, 1961).

37. Bernard of Clairvaux, "Office of St. Victor," in *Treatises* I (Cistercian Fathers Series, 1970).

38. For analyses of medieval church councils, see Dom H. Leclercq, *Histoire des Conciles* (1907–1921).

39. See, for example, Ruth H. Cline, "The Influence of Romances on Tournaments of the Middle Ages," *Speculum* (April 1945), pp. 204–11.

40. Chandos Herald, *Life of the Black Prince*, p. 150.

41. *Sir Gawain and the Green Knight*, trans. Marie Borroff (New York, 1967), line 640.

42. Gervase Matthew, *The Court of Richard II*, pp. 125–27.

43. N. Denholm-Young, *History and Heraldry, 1254–1310* (Oxford, 1965), p. 5.

44. Barker, *The Tournament in England*, pp. 104–6.

45. See Chapter 7 in this volume: J. K. Rühl, "Sports Quantification in Tudor and Elizabethan Tournaments."

46. Georges Duby, *William Marshal: The Flower of Chivalry*, trans. Richard Howard (New York, 1985), p. 94. See also P. Meyer, ed., *Histoire de Guillaume le Maréchal*, 3 vols. (Paris, 1891–1901). Probably the definitive study of the Marshal is Sidney Painter's *William Marshal* (Baltimore, 1933). Also valuable is Jessie Crosland, *William the Marshal: The Last Great Feudal Baron* (London, 1962). Useful for the military operations in Anglo-Norman and early Angevin England is John Beeler's *Warfare in England, 1066–1189* (Ithaca, N.Y., 1966).

47. Duby, *William Marshal*, pp. 102–6.

48. *Histoire de Guillaume le Maréchal*, 11. 18481–96. The English translation is given in Antonia Gransden, *Historical Writing in England, ca. 550–ca. 1307* (Ithaca, N.Y., 1974), p. 350.

49. Duby, *William Marshal*, pp. 28–29.

50. Ibid.

51. Gilbert Marshal's death is recorded in Matthew Paris's thirteenth-century chronicle, *Chronica majora*. I found this citation in N. Denholm-Young's *History and Heraldry*, p. 73.

6

The Numbers of Reason: Luck, Logic, and Art in Renaissance Conceptions of Sport

JOHN McCLELLAND

On June 29, 1443, the city of Lucca, in the plain of Tuscany, founded an annual crossbow competition.[1] The purpose was essentially a military one. Lucca had won independence from its larger neighbors, Pisa and Florence, in 1369, but had to rely on a citizens' militia for defense against possible subsequent incursions. The competitions seem to have been an enticement to encourage young Luccans to undergo the ''months of training required to use the crossbow effectively'' (Dupuy, 1980:91) and to maintain their skills at an appropriate level. It was perhaps to that end that the competitions were made to look like sport by being called *ludi* (games) rather than *exercitationes* (training) and that prizes were awarded with a specified monetary value.[2] So as to ensure that the winner really was the best shot and to prevent any competitor from taking unfair advantage, the decrees also stipulated an obligatory firing line 120 *passi* (89 meters) from the targets.

Except for the fact that the Lucca competition seems better organized than similar archery contests that had flourished in Europe since the thirteenth century (see, e.g., Burgener 1980), there is almost nothing in these rules that might surprise us, either from the historical point of view or from our modern conception of the criteria of a valid competition. The decrees even provide for a means of settling arguments between contestants. Since all the archers fired simultaneously at the same target—that at least is what we deduce from the rules—each competitor had to inscribe his name on his arrows (or, more properly, bolts), thus avoiding confusion on the part of the judges.

The rules go on to add a stipulation that reminds us that their authors conceived of sport in terms that remain very different from ours. Should it happen that one bolt strike another already embedded in the target and thereby destroy it and make the archer's name illegible, the prize would be awarded to the second archer. The first would have to blame not the injustice inherent in the rules but his own bad luck (*fortuna*).

The *fortuna* invoked here is not the divinity who in the Middle Ages had embodied what we now call acts of God, but rather the personal luck of the archer, the counterpart of his skill. This patent injustice that the rules themselves admit exists could, of course, easily have been remedied. Separate targets for each shooter could have been set up; or the archers could have fired consecutively, with a note made of the position of each bolt in relation to the bulls-eye. By specifying in the rules that situations might arise over which the judges would leave the decision to chance, the drafters of the Lucca competition abdicated what now seems the normal responsibility of any bureaucracy whose function is to regulate sporting events: to ensure that luck does not fundamentally alter the "equality in the conditions of competition" that is a *sine qua non* of modern sport (Guttmann 1978, 15–16, 28–29). The Lucca contest was not in any sense ritualistic.[3] Yet by stating that the principle of equality could be applied to a certain extent and no further, the rules can be seen to combine two antithetical conceptions of sport, one of which would disappear in the succeeding 150 years.

At first glance the Lucca crossbow competition seems to resemble similar efforts on the part of other Italian municipal governments to intervene in traditional secular games. William Heywood's classic *Palio and Ponte* (1904) recounts the cities' successive attempts to regulate the quasi-athletic confrontations that had sporadically set districts or other constituted groups one against the other. By the late thirteenth century the more dangerous of these began to be abolished (e.g., the *battaglia de' sassi*, or stone fight, in Perugia), whereas others, thought to be closely identified with the character and fortunes of the city, were subjected to various forms of rationalization. The course of the Siena *palio*, which had originally been run through the streets of the city, was measured and then recalculated as a number of circuits of the central Piazza del Campo. In that way, the horse race which every August 15th reasserted Siena's consecration to the Virgin Mary became visible to the largest possible number of citizens (Heywood 1904, 212; Dundes and Falassi 1975, 8).[4] In the case of the Pisa "bridge game" (*giuoco del ponte*), the government gradually reduced the length of the encounters, established norms with which the weapons had to comply, and set down rules concerning the roles and functions of the various players (Heywood 1904, 93–137). In Florence the type of rugby football known as *calcio* was also closely supervised.[5]

Generally speaking, town councils were attempting, if not to eliminate, at least to contain the violence that was endemic in these "games," in which fatal accidents were frequent. In so doing, they hoped to channel traditional, divisive rivalries into imitations of the former games. These imitations would be less violent, and therefore less harmful to the social fabric, because they were directed to more symbolic and less physical ends. In Siena, for example, the *palio* came to replace a whole series of other sports such as the *pugna* (or fistfight) and the *bufalata* (buffalo baiting) (Dundes and Falassi 1975, 5).[6] In Florence *calcio* players were required to exhaust their animosities on the field, under "payne of death," according to an English traveler (Lassels 1670, 212–15).[7]

The town councils' efforts to reduce violence also produced side effects. The first of these came about from the application of a military analogy to team sports. As a result, many of these games (e.g., *ponte*) ceased to be disorderly free-for-alls and came to look more like pitched battles. Players' roles tended to become specialized, and the outcome was increasingly determined on the basis of arithmetic and geometrical principles. *Calcio* provides, perhaps, the clearest example of this process.

Though played in many cities of Northern Italy, *calcio* was a game the Florentines liked to think of as their own. As early as 1465, Giovanni Frescobaldi had composed a long poem of a slightly patriotic flavor that recounts in precise detail, including the names of all the players, a game between two fifteen-men teams at the Piazza Santo Spirito (Lanza 1973–75, 1:601–7). (The game seemed to end as soon as the first goal was scored.) Contemporary documents tell us that *calcio* was played in any convenient open space, including the ice of the frozen Arno in January 1490 (see Masi 1906). However, the *prato*, a meadow bounded by the city wall (*muro*) and the protective moat (*fossa*), was a favorite place—so much so that the two sides of the field retained those designations even when the game was played elsewhere. By 1565 the large rectangular Piazza Santa Croce had become the most common venue for the matches, so that permanent marble plaques were set into the facades of facing buildings to indicate the midfield stripe. (One of these plaques is still in place today.)

When Giovanni Maria Bardi came to write his treatise expounding the ideal standard form of *calcio* (Bardi 1580), the game was no longer spontaneous and disorderly, but required careful preparation and set times and dates. Bardi's little book is extraordinarily precise on a number of points: (1) the tactical functions of each of the four groups of players (fifteen forwards, five blockers, four front-line punters, three rear-line punters) including some distinctions within each group;[8] (2) the initial arrangement of the players—they line up to replicate the Roman order of battle—and the exact distances that separate them (e.g., the "moat-side blocker" is to stand eleven *braccia* from the side-line, twenty-three *braccia* behind the forwards, sixteen from the blocker on his left, and eighteen ahead of the front-line punters [one *braccio* = 0.58 meters]); (3) the dimensions of the playing field: 172×86 *braccia* or $\pm\ 100 \times 50$ meters[9] (4) the fact that the team that scores more points wins the game (in view of Bardi's explicitness on this subject, one gathers that this is an innovation); (5) the permissible duration of a game, which Bardi expresses in a combination of sun and clock time (Bardi 1580 in Bascetta 1978; 1:139–43, 161).

Before Bardi, *calcio* was a "qualified" game in which victory was factored by the quality of play displayed by the two teams, as determined by the judges, who observed the game from special stands. By imposing on *calcio* a measurement system enunciated in precise numbers, Bardi made it into a partially quantified sport. His rules eliminate the unpredictable effects of the judges' possibly subjective decisions; of any team's failure to develop a territorial strategy; of a field size that might be unfamiliar to one team or the other; of any form of favoritism in putting the ball into play; or of wind direction and sunlight, since the teams changed ends after every point. Unlike the Lucca rules, Bardi's specify that the judges will decide those cases that are not explicitly covered. Insofar as is possible, Bardi leaves nothing to chance.[10]

Popular and semipopular team sports were not the only ones to be affected by bureaucratic intervention. When the duke of Milan arranged a joust in May 1465, his civil servants drew up a list of twenty-two rules (Angelucci 1866) whose apparent purpose was identical to those of the Lucca decrees. Individual competitors were to be prevented from taking unfair advantage by the fact that their saddles and lances had to conform to established standards. The scoring system awarded a specific number of points for each feat—one point for striking your opponent in the head, two points for striking him in the head and unhorsing him, and so on—so that the winner was indisputably the knight who had amassed the most points. As in the case of Bardi's *calcio* rules, but again unlike Lucca, it is stipulated that the judges will decide any cases not covered by the rules. Although a contemporary hand crossed out some of these rules, adding a note to the effect that no one would obey them, the intention remains clear: to ensure that the winner owes his victory to his talent alone and not to some material advantage, subjective judgment, or foreseeable chance.

The chief concern of the authors of the texts we have been examining has been to impose on certain games an order that had theretofore been lacking. In all cases, this order is based on a system of exact measurements that delimit the playing space, fix the dimensions of any apparatus (clubs, lances, saddles, etc.), determine the length of the game, regulate the number of players, and establish a numerical system of scoring. The imposition of measurement and order entails concomitantly the elimination of chance as a factor influencing the course of play or its result. Bardi insisted that *calcio* be played *con ragione* (literally "with reason"), but this term then and now has strong mathematical connotations. For example, *ragioniere* means "accountant."

Other sports were the subject of less official but no less important attempts at incipient quantification. As early as 1537 Francesco Altoni tried to restructure fencing along the mathematical lines we have observed in other sports. He boasts of being the first to treat fencing "in an orderly fashion, demonstrating its principles and reducing it to universals." He considers it an art based on prior conceptualization and not a mere game (*giuoco*) as his predecessors had called it, notably Marozzo (1536) (Altoni 1537, 4r°).[11] The fencer's *en garde* stance (the relative positions of his head, arms, sword, and feet) must be encompassed within a circle drawn on the ground, whose diameter must equal two-thirds of a man's height. All thrusts, parries, and other gestures and movements are measured in terms of the height and step of a well-proportioned individual. To be sure, these measurements are not arithmetical but geometric and therefore relative and, to a certain extent, flexible. In the course of the match the geometry of the initial circle may be modified into an oval, but these variations must be within one-third and five-twelfths of a man's height. Altoni's stated goal is to reach a "very certain knowledge" of fencing (13v°) and to transform it into a kind of "architecture" to be performed by a "self-controlled and wise" man whose bodily movements are dominated by his knowledge and reason (24r°–26r°).

Camillo Agrippa (1553), who may have seen Altoni's unpublished treatise, continued the process of establishing a mathematical order for fencing. His book analyzes the succession of body and sword gestures by applying to them a set of geometrical figures that vary with the movements of the limbs (ff. A3r°, A4v°, Blv°, etc.). Agrippa stresses that the exercise of fencing "is exclusively regulated by points, lines, tempos, measures, and such like, and these arise so to speak from mathematical, or more simply, geometrical considerations" (A3r°).[12]

The writers we have been referring to make no explicit mention of "luck" or "chance" or "fortune." The concepts of order, measurement, and mathematical reason that they are keen to apply are presented as unquestioned absolutes, even though it is clear that they envisage these concepts as replacing something else. Antonio Scaino's book on ball games (1555)—especially tennis—differs in this respect from other Renaissance sports books. The text bristles with numbers: dimensions of the small and large tennis courts, sizes of the various types of racquets and paddles, diameters and weights of different kinds of balls.[13] These are all measurements that Scaino considers to be inviolable and invariable. He calls tennis an "exceedingly reasonable" game; to play it requires "intelligence and technique" rather than "Fortune and luck." That is why the minimum margin of victory must be four points (i.e., 4–0, 5–1, etc.), since any single point might be the result of chance (Scaino 1555, II, 4–6, 16–18, 21–22). He later adds that because *pallacorda*—one of the six varieties of tennis—is an "excellent and noble" game, victory must not depend on "fortuitous accidents" (quoted from Bascetta 1978, 2:291).

On the other hand, the walls of enclosed tennis courts were not flat surfaces. Openings, overhangs, and columns were frequent, and these features were not symmetrically distributed in the two halves of the court.[14] Scaino seems to be pleased that "so many lovely accidents" can occur during a game as a result of these irregularities, but though he appears to be contradicting his earlier assertion, he is in fact not doing so. For these chance effects that cause the spectators "astonishment and pleasure" are completely under control of the "discerning and skillful player." The "accidents" that can alter the course of a game are but the appearances of chance or luck and do not violate the overriding reason and order that dominate the sport.

Scaino has, however, posited two levels of perception. On the level of the spectators, events appear to be dictated by chance; on the level of the players and the cognoscenti, events are produced by skill and intelligence and are dictated by abstract quasimathematical reasoning. A slightly later text makes this double level more explicit.

Pino. . . . In addition to performing gracefully, Signor Battista measured out his feat so exactly and proportionately and timed it so accurately that at the end of a sequence of reverse handsprings he executed a back flip over a garter that two men were holding as high as they could at the end of the room. This tour de force mightily pleased and satisfied the spectators. His somersault rather more resembled a windmill turning than a human body.

Battista. Inasmuch as I know you would enjoy knowing the precise ratios I establish in order to perform any given number of reverse handsprings, you must realize that, unbeknownst to those present, I silently pace off the distance in a straight line from where the garter is to be held to where I want to begin the first handspring, counting two steps for one handspring. By measuring in that way, I never fail to finish right in front of the garter before somersaulting over it.

This passage is drawn from Arcangelo Tuccaro's three dialogues on tumbling (1599, 84r° − v°). Like the author of most Renaissance sports manuals, Tuccaro never speaks of fortune, chance, or luck. His purpose is also the same as theirs: to structure mat gymnastics by imposing a system of geometrical measurement. A large number of the eighty-eight woodcuts that illustrate the book show circles and straight lines superimposed on the picture of the gymnast. These represent the arcs that his body will describe between the initial and final vertical stances. Like Altoni, Tuccaro thinks of each of the fifty-four acrobatic feats his book analyzes as a "piece of architecture" whose elements are proportionate to each other. Before the body performs them, the mind must have properly conceived them (Tuccaro 1599, 2r°, 6r°, etc.).

Tuccaro's meaning is just as unambiguous as that of the earlier manuals. In sport, nothing must be left to chance. Whoever trusts to luck is lost beforehand. But by the same token, the spectators must not be aware of all the practical, intellectual, mathematical preparation that has preceded the performance of every feat. They must believe that success depends on phenomena that are out of the ordinary, and among these, fortune and chance, which the successful athlete will have enlisted as allies.

The process that can be observed in Renaissance sports manuals and bureaucratic decrees is part of a larger intellectual pattern. Between 1300 and 1600 the tendency in all branches of purposeful human activity lay in the direction of an increasing reliance on quasi-objective systems of measurement, on what Robert Klein called the "mathématisation de la nature" (Klein 1970, 333). Generally speaking, measurement replaced a kind of pragmatics of performance or creation in which problems (e.g., perspective in painting, metrics in music) had been solved on an *ad hoc* basis. Both serendipity and a rather arbitrary symbolism were major factors in the solution of difficulties. In areas of theological significance—the building and decoration of churches—success could be attributed to the visitations of the Holy Spirit. In secular activities it was Fortuna who intervened.

Whatever the reasons for the dissatisfaction with Christian and allegorical explanations of causality, the impulse toward the rationalization that is implied by measurement is just as real in Renaissance sports as it is in Renaissance science. Measurement, of course, means quantification: the expression of any entity as a multiple of some unit that may or may not be—but usually is—extrinsic to the entity in question. To relate an entity to a unit is to create a mathematical *ratio* of the type n:1, to reduce the entity to the status of a phenomenon susceptible of being comprehended by the reason (Latin *ratio*), not merely apprehended intuitively by the critical judgement. To quantify *calcio* or fencing or tumbling in the manner Bardi and Altoni and Tuccaro suggest is perhaps not so much a way of changing the practice of these sports as a way of making their performance comprehensible to their practitioners.

Measurement and quantification require, of course, concepts, standards, and instruments that are adequate to the entities that are their object. Conversely, entities may come into being simply because there are ways of measuring them. Of the sports we have been examining, only archery contests, fencing, and mat gymnastics still survive. *Ponte, calcio*, and most forms of Scaino's tennis have gone the way of jousting, whereas *palio* lost any sporting significance in the seventeenth century. On the other hand, we have made no mention of running, throwing, jumping, swimming, weightlifting, and so forth, of which are the foundations of the *citius-altius-fortius* creed and of the modern Olympics.[15] From the writings of those who in the Renaissance touched directly or indirectly on the subject of education we know that all these sports were practiced, but almost exclusively from the point of view of physical exercise and military training. There seems to have been competition in some of these sports among schoolboys. Montaigne tells us in his *Essais* (Bk II, ch. 17) that there was scarcely anyone who did not better him in all forms of bodily exercise, "except in running (at which I was fairly average)." Swimming, in spite of some initial repugnance among the upper classes, became more widely accepted and practiced during the sixteenth century, but as paintings and contemporary manuals inform us (e.g., Digby 1587), its purpose was largely recreational and the main concern was learning how to stay afloat (Krüger 1984). Although neophyte swimmers were encouraged to emulate Julius Caesar's example of swimming 200 meters with his cloak in his teeth and holding important documents out of the water, there seems to have been no notion of swimming races.

Outside of school, contests of strength and speed may have flourished among rustics, but the only recorded footraces were held in conjunction with Carnival; and these involved only outcast and marginalized social groups, such as prostitutes and others. Thus, during the Roman carnival of 1581 Montaigne erected a scaffold on the Corso to observe among other things footraces involving children, Jews, and naked old men (Montaigne [1580–1581]; 206). Although prizes were awarded to the winners, footraces were clearly associated with animal baiting and other manifestations that signified scorn and ridicule for beings that dwelt on society's fringes (see also Burke 1978, 184–88).

Something as naturally quantifiable as contests of strength and speed remained excluded from Renaissance sports in the first instance for social reasons. But in the second instance, they may have been excluded for reasons related to the stage of quantification that sport in the Renaissance was capable of attaining. Footraces are measured in order to produce a ratio of time over distance. It makes sense to record these ratios only if they are going to be compared to other ratios. Measuring short distances in the Renaissance was no problem, but the units of measurement were always strictly local. We have seen above that in Lucca space was divided into steps, whereas Bardi preferred *braccia* ("arm-lengths") and Scaino's favorite measure was the Roman foot. There was thus no means of comparing footraces from one locality to the next.

More importantly, in the absence of portable, accurate, sophisticated watches, there was no means of timing races so as to compare achievements. It is believed that Galileo could time phenomena down to one-twenty-fifth of a second, but whatever his apparatus, it was not available to the sporting world. There was hence no way of rationalizing footraces; they all remained *ad hoc* isolated events. Hence, there was no way of incorporating them into the realm of sport. Though not affected by timing, weightlifting and jumping, like running, suffered from the local nature of all forms of measurement. In addition, they were disparaged because of a gentlemanly distaste for displays of brute strength, even though they might be good military exercise.

To sum up, Renaissance sports stand astride a nexus of competing and often contradictory intellectual and social trends. Although the individual is increasingly being identified as the sum of his own qualities and potentialities, and not just as a member of a family, clan, guild, or other social order, new forms of pressure are curbing his impulse toward an egotistical untrammeled assertion of his wishes and his personality. To win an athletic contest you must first submit to measurable standards that are the same for all; you must win within the rules.

Violence and atrocities continue to be common in warfare and in judicial uses. But in addition to a growing revulsion against these practices in the name of humanity and Christianity, there is also a sense that violence should only be exerted against the outsider: the criminal, the witch, the apostate, the foreign enemy. The sense of community is growing larger and with it the feeling that to hurt a member of one's community is to weaken the ties that bind. If victory can be determined by a number of goals rather than by the number of dead bodies, broken limbs and bloody noses, no permanent harm will have been done.

Although Renaissance medicine was still bogged down in biochemical conceptions that dated from the Romans and a neurology that had not evolved further since Plato and Aristotle, enormous progress had been made in anatomy. Altoni, Agrippa, Scaino, and Tuccaro were fully aware of the body's skeletal and muscular possibilities. They understood biomechanical effects—why a thrust or serve or handspring would succeed if the body was first set in a certain posture and moved in certain ways. Their internal explanations of causes, however, seem flawed and superstitious. By appealing to geometrical descriptions, they can situate causality on the level of abstract universals. Although Tuccaro himself admits that an acrobat's body does not really describe geometrical figures (f. 68r°), by pretending that it does he can explain the art of performing physically unusual feats as an intellectual process modeled on an extrinsic system of order. Quantification in this case replaces a physiology that has not yet been imagined.

Finally, quantification is a code, a private language and system of thought, in which the athlete articulated his technique. Much of Renaissance sport was either pure professional spectacle or, in the case of fencing, of individual instruction whose worth was based on its superiority to rival methods and pedagogies. In both cases secrecy was essential. It is significant that virtually all Renaissance sports manuals were written by elderly athletes in such desperate need of money that they were willing to reveal that their art depended on a few mathematical calculations. Whereas, in contrast to the Middle Ages, Renaissance aesthetic theory had developed an extensive body of technical precepts, it had also enunciated the notion that the art of art consists in concealing art. By applying quantifying principles, however rudimentarily adumbrated, for spectators who were mathematically naive (as almost all Renaissance people were), athletes were simply extending the principles of art theory to sports.

In the Renaissance mathematics was a spatial discipline. Operations like multiplication were conducted geometrically and were therefore understood as complex ratios of line segments rather than as arithmetical manipulations of absolute numbers. Geometry, as anyone who has studied Euclid knows, is an art of reasoning, a mode of thought that proceeds from propositions to proofs with the aid of axioms and other previously established proofs. Its purpose is to demonstrate that, however complex a configuration may be, the mind has a means for grasping and describing it in real, not symbolic, terms. The Middle Ages had displayed a strong suspicion of the body and its impulses—though perhaps not as strong as commonplace belief would like to imagine (see Körbs 1938). By attempting to demonstrate that at least some games and physical exercises could be ordered along the same rational mathematical lines that were being adopted in other areas, Renaissance athletes and sporting enthusiasts were, in addition to other ends, seeking to confer on sport its *lettres de noblesse*. Being by its very nature a spatial activity, sport naturally lent itself to geometrical quantification. Perhaps the unstated hope that lay behind this preliminary quantification of sport was that the presence of numbers and lines would make the actions and gestures of individuals and teams not only seem but actually be logical. As everywhere else, the shadows of Descartes and Galileo were looming over the playing field.

NOTES

1. In 1487, after the invention of the harquebus, a firearms competition was added. See Angelucci, 1863:38 ff. and Appendix xxv-xxxi for an account of these decrees and a transcription of the text.

2. As was customary in Italy at this time, the prizes took the form of pieces of cloth, though the second prize for the harquebus competition was a gun. Contestants in the harquebus competition had to own their own gun and have had some previous training in firing it (*personas ad id instructas*). Initially, there had to be a minimum of twenty competitors, but this number was later raised to sixty.

3. By this I mean that the competition had no religious side to it; the only value in participating lay in the degree of success achieved. The competition was open to anyone, and it was not a folk game whose origins lay in some myth or legend. (See Guttmann, 1978 for the basis of this definition.)

4. In 1581 the French writer Michel de Montaigne reported that the *palio* in Florence, which was still run through the streets, was not an agreeable spectacle because the spectators could only observe a few horses racing madly past (Montaigne [1580–1581], 308).

5. In modern Italian *calcio* simply means soccer. In the Renaissance game, which was played by fifteen to twenty-seven players to a side, the ball could be carried or struck by the hand, though kicking was the preferred method of propulsion.

6. On the *palio* see also Handelman, 1984. In 1425 Gentile Sermini wrote a vivid, blow-by-blow account of *pugna* that stresses its boisterous roughhouse character; see Vettori (ed.) 1968, 1:193–97.

7. An early sixteenth-century scholar—he called himself "Filopono" (almost literally, "workaholic") but his real name was Stefano di Francesco Sterponi—described a *calcio* match in 1514, shortly after he arrived in Florence to take up a position at the University (Nardini 1898). What seemed to impress him most was the fighting among the players and among the spectators. In the tiny Vicolo de' Cavallari in Florence one can still see a plaque affixed in 1669 forbidding all manner of ball games in the immediate neighborhood. The punishment was a fine and two days in jail. The concern seems to have been violence rather than simply noise.

8. Bardi also specifies that each position on the team corresponds to a precise physical type. Thus, for example, the "wall-side blocker" must be the strongest, heaviest limbed player on the team.

9. Although these dimensions correspond to the size of the Piazza Santa Croce, Bardi does not mention this square or any other as a preferred playing field, thereby stressing the noncontingent nature of his rules.

10. The bibliography of *calcio* is considerable. In addition to Frescobaldi and Filopono, Antonio Scaino had written on *calcio* before Bardi, in his treatise on ball games (1555). Bardi's *Discorso* was republished in 1615 and 1673—the 1673 edition also contains a succinct, itemized version of the rules and a schematic plan of the teams in "kick-off" position, both derived from Bardi. Bini's compendium of materials on *calcio* (1688) reprints the 1673 edition and adds an engraving showing the start of a game. (See Heywood, 1904 and McClelland, 1985 for a reproduction.) Among the many modern writers on the game, one need retain only Lensi (1931) and Artusi and Gabbrielli (1971), in addition, of course, to Heywood.

11. Altoni's manuscript is actually undated, but textual evidence suggests that it was written in the latter part of 1537. All translations from Italian and French sources here and elsewhere are mine.

12. Later writers such as Dall'Agocchie (1572) and Docciolini (1601) extend and refine the principles first enunciated by Altoni and Agrippa.

13. Under the general heading of *palla* (Ital. for "ball"), Scaino studies not only the varieties of tennis, but also *calcio* and games that were ancestors of volleyball.

14. The original tennis courts seem to have been castle or monastery courtyards. Such spaces naturally feature doorways, windows, projecting roofs, and the like. When courts began to be designed and built solely for playing purposes, formerly functional details were incorporated into them because they had become part of the game. (See De Luze 1933).

15. For reasons of time and space we have similarly omitted any reference to dressage and to horse vaulting, though there exists an ample and important Renaissance literature of these subjects. (See Bascetta 1978.)

REFERENCES

Agrippa, Camillo 1553. *Trattato di scientia d'arme*. Rome: Antonio Blado.

Altoni, Francesco. 1537. Monomachia ovvero arto di scherma. MS. Florence.

Angelucci, Angelo. 1863. *Il tiro a segno in Italia dal XII al XVI secolo. Cenni storici con documenti inediti*. Turin: Baglione.

———. 1866. *Armilustre e torneo* . . . . Turin: Cassone.

Artusi, Luciano, and Silvano Gabbrielli. 1971. *L'antico giuoco del calcio in Firenze*. Florence: Sansoni.

Bardi, Giovanni. 1580. *Discorso sopra il giuoco del calcio fiorentino*. Vol. 1 of *Sport e giuochi,* ed. c. Bascetta, 131–62. Milan: Il Polifilo.

Bascetta, Carlo, ed. 1978. *Sport e giuochi*. 2 vols. Milan: Il Polifilo.

Bini, Pietro di Lorenzo. 1688. *Memorie del calcio fiorentino*. Florence: Nella Stamperia di S.A.S. alla Condotta.

Burgener, Louis. 1980. Games and Physical Exercises in Switzerland in the 15th and 16th Centuries. *Olympic Review* 162:237–40.

Burke, Peter. 1978. *Popular Culture in Early Modern Europe*. London: Temple Smith.

Dall'Agocchie, Giovanni. 1572. *Dell'arte di scrimia*. Venice: G. Tamborino.

Digby, Everard. 1587. *De arte natandi*. London: T. Dawson.

Docciolini, Marco. 1601. *Trattato in materia di scherma*. Florence: M. Sermartelli.

Dundes, Alan, and Alessandro Falassi. 1975. *La Terra in Piazza: An Interpretation of the Palio of Siena*. Berkeley and Los Angeles: University of California Press.

Dupuy, Trevor N. 1980. *The Evolution of Weapons and Warfare*. New York: Bobbs-Merrill.

Guttmann, Allen. 1978. *From Ritual to Record: The Nature of Modern Sports*. New York: Columbia University Press.

Handelman, Don. 1984. Die Madonna und die Stute: Zur symbolischen Bedeutung des Palio von Siena. In *Die Anfänge des modernen Sports in der Renaissance*, eds. Krüger and McClelland, 58–84. London: Arena Publications.

Heywood, William. 1904. *Palio and Ponte: The Sports of Central Italy from the Age of Dante to the XXth Century*. London: Methuen; New York: Hacker, 1967.

Huizinga, Johan. 1939. *Homo ludens. Versuch einer Bestimmung des Spielelementes der Kultur*. Amsterdam: Pantheon.

Klein, Robert. 1970. *La forme et l'intelligible. Ecrits sur la Renaissance et l'art moderne*. Paris: Gallimard.

Körbs, Werner. 1938. *Vom Sinn der Leibesübungen zur Zeit der italienischen Renaissance*. Berlin: Weidmann.

Krüger, Arnd. 1984. Schwimmen: Der Wandel in der Einstellung zu einer Form der Leibesübungen. In *Die Anfänge des modernen Sports in der Renaissance,* eds. Krüger and McClelland, 19–42. London: Arena Publications.

Krüger, Arnd, and John McClelland. 1984. *Die Anfänge des modernen Sports in der Renaissance.* London: Arena Publications.

Lanza, Antonio, ed. 1973. *Lirici toscani del '400.* 2 vols. Rome: Bulzoni.

Lassels, Richard. 1670. *The Voyage of Italy.* Paris: Vincent du Moutier.

Lensi, Alfredo. 1931. *Il giuoco del calcio fiorentino.* Florence: Rinascimento del libro.

Luze, Albert de. 1933. *La magnifique histoire du jeu de paume.* Paris: Brossard; Bordeaux: Delmas.

Marozzo, Achille. 1536. *Opera nova chiamata duello.* Modène: A. Bergola.

Masi, Bartolomeo. 1906. *Ricordanze (1478–1526).* Edited by G. O. Corazzini. Florence: Sansoni.

McClelland, John. 1985. Sport et spectacle à la Renaissance. *Théâtre/Public* 63:20–24.

Montaigne, Michel de. [1580–81]. *Journal de voyage.* Edited by F. Garavini. Folio; Paris: Gallimard, 1983.

Nardini, C., ed. 1898. *Filopono, Il giuoco del calcio.* Florence: Carnesecchi.

Scaino, Antonio. 1550. *Trattato del giuoco della palla.* Venise: G. Giolito de'Ferrari.

Tuccaro, Arcangelo. 1599. *Trois dialogues de l'exercise de sauter et voltiger en l'air.* Paris: Claude de Monstr'oeil.

Vettori, Giuseppe, ed. 1968. *Gentile Sermini, Novelle.* 2 vols. Rome: Avanzini e Torraca.

7

Sports Quantification in Tudor and Elizabethan Tournaments

JOACHIM RÜHL

On the first anniversary of Queen Elizabeth I's accession to the throne, on November 17, 1559, Sir Henry Lee (1530–1610), then clerk of the armoury and a "model knight," [1] made a vow that he would each year challenge all comers.[2] His purpose was to maintain the queen's honor, who in turn gladly accepted his chivalrous offer, nominating him to be her champion. Lee inaugurated the Society of Knights Tilters acting himself as this society's president. As the queen's personal champion he also started the spectacular series of the Accession Day Tournaments, having been the main challenger for exactly thirty years when he resigned office on November 17, 1590. His successor was George Clifford, third earl of Cumberland.[3]

Before we can deal with the Accession Day Tournaments, however, which was a regular event in the courtly calendar, we have to go back nearly a century to understand the method of scoring employed in those days.

Tradition has it that it was the office of the ladies and gentlewomen to hand out the prizes to the best jousters at the final banquet.[4] In a manuscript collection of fifteenth-century copies we read:

Then comys forth a lady . . . & yevis þe Dyamund unto þe beste Juster . . . sayying in this wise. sere these ladiis & Gentill wymmen thank yow. for yowr dysport & yowr gret labur that ye have this day in thayre presens. and þe sayde ladiis and Gentyll wymmen sayyn þᵗ ye have beste Just this day. there fore þe sayde ladys & Gentyll-wymmen gyff yow this Diamunde & sende yow mych worschyp & ioye of yowr lady. Thus schall be doon wᵗ þe Rube & þe Sauffer. un to þe other ij nex best Justers this don.[5]

But it was not the ladies themselves who had actually done the scoring. They had been informed of the results by the heralds who immediately afterward confirmed the ladies' words: "Then schall ye harraude of arm^s stonde up all on hey & schall sey with a hey voyce. John hath well Justyd. Rycharde hath Justyd better. & Thom^{a}s hath Justyd best of all."[6] After this official statement of the herald, the best jouster took the lady by the hand, thus opening the dance. The lady had no idea how many lances her partner had broken during the several events of the preceding tournament.

When Lord Scales officially challenged the Bastard of Burgundy in the year 1446, John Tiptofte, earl of Worcester and constable of England, was asked to draw up the Ordinances For Justes of Peace Royal which would regulate scoring in the joust or tilt for more than a century to come. As Tiptofte's Rules are dealt with in detail elsewhere,[7] let us briefly summarize what he had laid down. When two knights rode against one another the breaking of the lance between the opponent's saddle and the charnel, the bolt holding the helmet (cf. illustration 1) counted one point.

If the lance was broken above the bolt, he earned two points. Three points were scored when the opponent was unseated, when he was disarmed, or when the top ("coronel") of the lance was hit. Tiptofte's Rules also knew of forfeitures of points. One point was lost when the lance was broken on the opponent's saddle, striking the tilt or plank that separated the knights once cost two points, and striking it twice cost three. A mere "attaint," a touch, on the body was less than a point; an attaint on the visor scored two points. (Several regulations of minor importance must be omitted here.) In later times attaints on the head were marked by a stroke *on* the head-line, a lance broken on the head by a stroke transsecting the head-line. This also applied to the middle or body-line. Forfeitures were marked on the lowest line but are very rarely found in the records of the heralds. On the extended middle line we find the number of "courses" or charges entered (cf. illustration 2). Keeping such records had always been the office of heralds and their pursuivants. It is in the encounter between Lord Scales and the Bastard of Burgundy in 1446 that we find such directions for the first time ever.[8] There is a similar notice for the year 1500 in Harl. Ms. no 326 on fol. 113^v and for June 1509 when Henry VIII's coronation was celebrated by a tournament held at Westminster. In that year the captain of the knights declared that the number of broken lances "by the viewe of the Iudges, and the report of the Herauldes," decided which party was to "haue the spere of Gold for their prise."[9]

We can only assume that such diagrams as the one in Exhibit 2 had already been in use in the second half of the fifteenth century, for it is not before the year 1501 that we actually come across a copy of the first list in which they are found. Such lists are called cheque-lists because they contain the cheques of the individual jousters with their scores entered. The marking was done by one of the heralds (cf. illustration 3).

On November 18, 1501 the duke of Buckingham proclaimed a challenge to

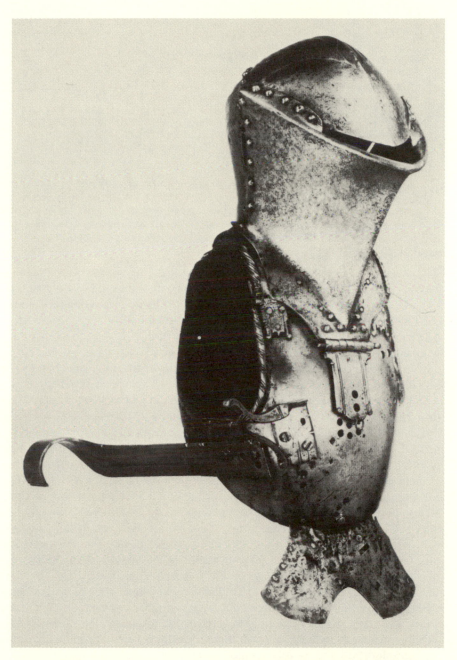

1. A rare German Gothic tilt armour of the second half of the fifteenth century showing the position of the charnel, the bolt fastening the helmet to the breastplate. Taken from *The Hever Castle Collection*, vol. 1 (Arms and Armour), illustrated catalogue. Sotheby's London 1983, p. 40, lot 45. Copyright Sotheby's, used by permission.

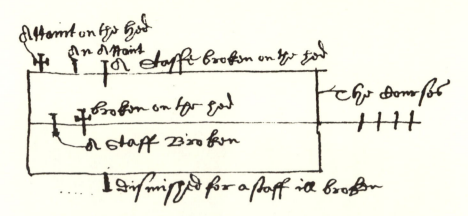

2. A sample cheque in the *Ordinances For Justes of Peace Royal* by John Tiptoft, Earl of Worcester, 1466. Taken from Ms Ashmole 763, fol 149ᵛ. Copyright The Bodleian Library Oxford, used by permission.

all comers to honor the marriage of Prince Arthur, the eldest son of King Henry VII, who was only fifteen years old at that time. The bride was fourteen-year-old Catherine of Aragon, the daughter of King Ferdinand II of Spain. She later married King Henry VIII (on June 11, 1509). A further reason for staging this tournament was, as the challengers stated, to perform "Exercise and faictes of the Necessary discipline of armes . . . to thenableing of Noblesse and chiualry," according to the "noble and laudable custome"[10] of England. A grand spectacle with thousands of spectators was prepared in the tilt-yard at Westminster. The lists were expected to be crowded by "grete nombres of nobles as wel [as] of this . . . realme as of other realmes and cuntreis . . . disposed and apte to knyghtly acts."[11] Contrary to the issued challenge, the tournament did not last for two days but had to be extended to four. The grouping of the challengers and answerers was fairly simple and arranged with the help of three trees (so-called tree-born challenges). The challengers, the duke of Buckingham, his brother Henry, Lord Berners, Sir Rowland de Vieilleville, and Sir George Herbert, hung their shields on an artificial cherry tree, either on its white side if they wanted to joust on the first day, or on its red side if on the second. The answerers in turn fastened their shields to a pineapple tree on the white side of the cherry tree to be served on the first day, or to the pear tree on the red side for the second. Heralds, pursuivants, and attendants were to stand close by to examine the shields presented and to record the names of the contestants in their lists which were later properly ruled out to enter the scores neatly. We do not know exactly whether everybody followed this procedure on the days following, for we are informed by two other sources[12] that on the actual day they ended up with only one tree and the shields of the contestants were hung all over the surrounding fence.

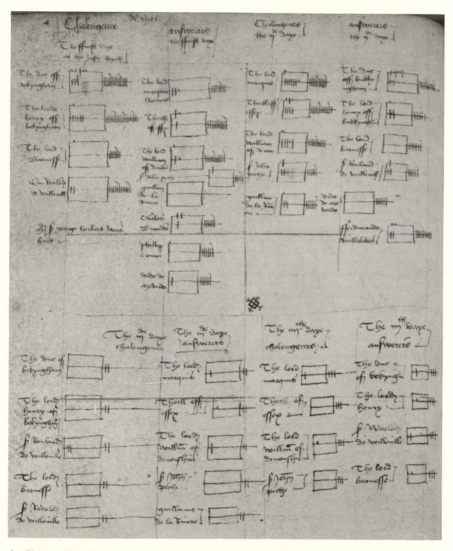

3. Cheque-list of the tournament in Westminster, held from 18 to 25 November 1501. Taken from The College of Arms Ms no. 3 (Ballard's Book), fol 25[b]. Copyright The College of Arms London, used by permission.

The scene of action was set, the tilt-yard sanded and strewn with gravel "to give the horses sure footing,"[13] and the tilt itself positioned in the middle. On the south side a richly decorated tilt-gallery was erected for the king, the queen, noblemen, and ladies. On the north side was a stage to seat the lord mayor of London and the dignitaries of the municipality. Surrounding the enclosed square were double stands with seats for the citizens and the common folk, which could be hired at "great price and costs."[14] Entrance fees for tournaments in Tudor times were exorbitant,[15] and fines for combatants failing to take part amounted to "some thousands of crowns"[16] in the year 1584. Guards and watchmen paraded all over the place preventing the access "of the rudes"[17] and ensuring that nobody disturbed the horses or ran into the piles of lances.

On the first day, Thursday, November 18, 1501, thousands of spectators pressed toward the lists. According to the herald's report, only "visages and faces"[18] could be seen, but no bodies belonging to them. When the spectacular parade of the tilters approached the lists, the heralds usually belonged to the first group. In those days they were called "Les Officiers darmes"; it was fashionable to use the French terminology. The onlookers were surprised by a kind of pageant never before witnessed. The duke of Buckingham rode his charger inside a pavilion, a tent of white and green silk. The answerers did not stand back: the marquis of Dorset rode in a golden pavilion, William Courtenay in a red dragon, Guillaume de Rivers in a huge ship, the earl of Essex in a green mountain, and Sir John Peche in a pavilion of red silk. This marked the introduction of fanciful pageantry into the Tudor tournament. After having stopped in front of the royal gallery, the combatants dismounted and got ready for the tilting. If we were to rely on the herald's report only, we would have learned of "such a feld, and justs ryall, so noble and valiantly doon [as] have not ben sen ne herd."[19] However, consulting the extant cheque-list (covering all the four days) for the first day, we realize that this was tantamount to a downright lie. For the standard of the jousters was very poor indeed (cf. illustration 3). On the left-hand side in the upper part of fol. 25^b of the College of Arms Ms M3 (Ballard's Book), we find the challengers arranged in the left column and the answerers in the right one. The list reads: "A° 1501. Challengeurs. answerers. The ffurst daye at the Justs Royall."

The entries for the four days have been enlarged so that the reader can easily follow the text (cf. illustration 4). In his seventeen courses or charges, the duke of Buckingham scored four attaints or touches on the head, one broken lance on the head, and three broken lances on the body. In ten charges he did not hit his opponent even once. In twenty charges his brother Henry scored one attaint on the head and five broken lances on the body. He missed completely in his other fourteen charges. Lord Berners rode only eight charges, scoring one single attaint on the head. Sir Rowland de Vieilleville broke only two lances on the body in his twelve charges. "Here Sir George Herbert was hurt" and had to give up.[20] The eight answerers did not fare any better: in their fifty-seven charges they scored three attaints on the head, four lances broken on the head, two attaints on the body, and six lances broken on the body. To sum up, both sides

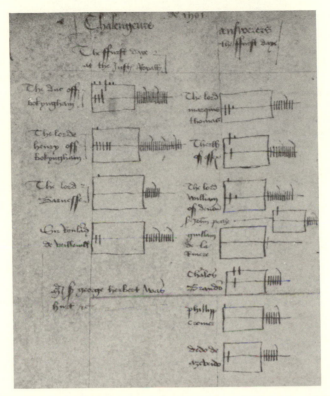

4. Cheque-list of the tournament in Westminster, held on 18 November 1501. En-larged section of ill. no. 3. Copyright The College of Arms London, used by permission.

ran fifty-seven charges, with the challengers missing in forty and the answerers in 42. It is interesting that a Spaniard, Dedo de Azeveido, was the last tilter on the side of the answerers.

The knights took a rest from Friday to Sunday and entered the tilt-yard for a second time with similar splendor on Monday, November 22, 1501. The rest must have served them well, for we notice a not inconsiderable improvement (cf. illustration 5). On this second day for reasons we cannot ascertain, the order of challengers and answerers was reversed. All in all, forty-eight charges were run. The challengers scored five attaints on the head, three lances broken on the head, two attaints on the body, and eighteen lances broken on the body, missing in only twenty charges. The answerers scored six attaints on the head, four lances broken on the head, one attaint on the body, and eight lances broken on the body, missing in twenty-nine charges. There was also a great difference in skill between the individual performers. In their twelve charges the marquis of Dorset scored eight hits, the duke of Buckingham had one more, and the earl of Essex

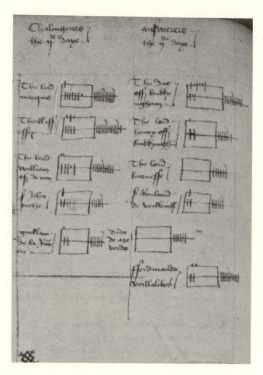

5. Cheque-list of the tournament in Westminster, held on 22 November 1501. Enlarged section of ill. no. 3. Copyright The College of Arms London, used by permission.

(in thirteen charges) ended up with seven. On the other hand, neither Lord Berners nor the Spaniard Dedo de Azeveido scored a single point in any of their charges. On this second day another Spaniard, Ferdinando Veillalobos, rode eleven charges scoring two attaints on the head and two lances broken on the body.

The combatants were granted another day's rest, and—contrary to the wording of the issued challenge—the tournament was resumed for a third time on Wednesday, November 14, 1501. As on the two days before, the participants entered the lists staging another spectacular pageant. Again the duke of Buckingham rode in his pavilion. The answerers (in French "Les Venants") had adorned their chargers with colorful horse trappings. The herald's report, however, again grossly exaggerates when stating that the sight was "so pleasurefull and so goodly that unto hit in tymys past have not beseene any like."[21] In reality, the spectators had witnessed two even more spectacular entries on the preceding two days. On the third day the separating tilt was removed and the ground was leveled and made even for the first part of this day's program: the running at large. In this rather dangerous discipline the knights ran against each other in

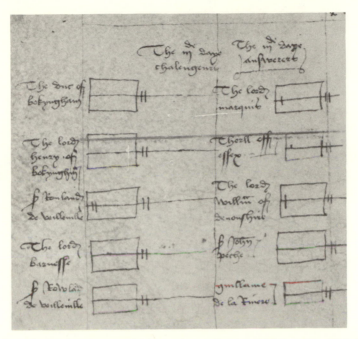

6. Cheque-list of the tournament in Westminster, held on 24 November 1501. Enlarged section of ill. no. 3. Copyright The College of Arms London, used by permission.

the open field carrying lances with sharp heads, so-called unrebaited spears (cf. illustration 6).

When consulting the cheque-list for the third day, we at once realize that running at large presented the riders with such risks that each of them rode only two charges (with one exception, see below). In view of the risks they were running, the knights seem to have been very very prudent and cautious. In the ten charges of the challengers only Sir Rowland de Vieilleville scored two lances broken on the body of Lord William of Devonshire. The answerers fared only slightly better. They scored two lances broken on the body and one attaint. All things taken together, there were only five hits in twenty charges, achieved by four knights. Six knights scored neither an attaint nor a broken lance. To give answerer number five a chance of competing, Sir Rowland de Vieilleville had to ride another two charges. Here again the report is not correct when it states that Sir Rowland "hadd the falle" in his encounter with Sir Henry. The cheques clearly tell us that it was impossible for them to have run against each other, because they belonged to the same side, to that of the challengers.

The second part of this day's program consisted of tourneying on horseback one against one. Swords with "rebaited" edges were used in this event. The report does not give any details, nor do we have a cheque-list with the scores

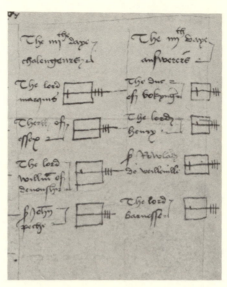

7. Cheque-list of the tournament in Westminster, held on 25 November 1501. Enlarged section of ill. no. 3. Copyright The College of Arms London, used by permission.

entered. Although the knights should have changed harness before resorting to the swords, we are not informed that they actually did so before the third part of the day. Although the knights changed harness, attendants erected a wooden barrier right in front of the king's tilt-gallery. When the challengers stood ready at the barrier, the answerers burst into the lists on a cart in the shape of a ship accompanied by the firing of guns and serpentines. The pageant stopped close to the gallery, the answerers "poured forth"[22] and without even saluting the dignitaries dashed toward the barrier. Here they first fought two against two across the barrier using their "spears" (probably shorter lances or halberds) striking with the point or with the butt-end. Then they all joined battle striking at each other dealing "hevy buffets and herde."[23]The cannon on board the ship was constantly fired, and the report affirmed that it was a "strange feat of armys, and goodliest that hath been seen."[24] We are not in a position to know whether or not this was true, for no cheque-list of this tilting at the barriers is available.

On the fourth and last day of the tournament, on Thursday, November 25, 1501, both sides followed by a large group of retainers paraded around the lists. (The barrier had been removed.) As on the second day the order of challengers and answerers was reversed, the marquis of Dorset leading the challengers on richly decorated horses. They surrounded a golden pageant car drawn by four fabulous beasts: two lions, one white and the other red, a golden horned hart, and an ibex. From the pageant car emerged "the inevitable fair young damsel''[25] who was *not* one of the prizes and who stepped up the tilt-gallery to join the ladies. This done, the first event on Thursday consisted of tilting on horseback in the open field, the combatants riding against each other one by one using ''coronels.'' There was no tilt separating the sides. As on the previous day each knight ran only three charges. Apparently, running at large, even with coronels, presented more dangers than jousting over the separating tilt. According to the cheque-list for this event (cf. illustration 7), the challengers in their twelve charges scored one attaint and one lance broken on the body. The answerers performed slightly better: they achieved two attaints and two lances broken on the body. The two Spaniards did not participate on the third and fourth days, that is, when the tilt had been removed. The last event on Thursday was a second tourney on horseback with swords. We are not sure whether these swords had rebaited edges or whether sharp weapons were being used. As there is no cheque-list for this event, we must rely on the report which says that challengers and answerers first fought against one and afterward five versus five. We hear of ''strykyng, rasyng and lasshyng at iche other many strokys, and longe season,'' of swords broken into pieces and of knights whose ''harneis was hewen off from their body, and [who] felle into the field.''[26] If this was true, it is possible that the swords had no rebaited edges or were not altogether blunt. However, we cannot be certain. Finally, the trumpets announced the end: ''A lhostel''—back to your lodgings. When the sun was setting, the challengers entered the pageant car, passed in front of the tilt-gallery, and, not forgetting to collect their beautiful damsel, left the tilt-yard for good. The ''Lyssue du Champ,'' the leaving of the tilt-yard, was the last parade. At the final banquet in Westminister Hall the duke of Buckingham was awarded the prize for the challengers: a diamond. The marquis of Dorset was given a ruby as the prize for the answerers. The rest received precious stones and gold rings. When we count the scores in all the extant cheques for the four days, these results are confirmed. The duke had scored eighteen hits, and the Marquis thirteen, closely followed by Lord William of Devonshire who came in with twelve. The heralds obviously had done their job well. After the banquet the parties ''made to their lodgyngs''[27] and Prince Arthur and Catherine of Aragon left for Ludlow in Wales on their honeymoon, where Prince Arthur died after a few months on April 2, 1502.

In Elizabethan times, that is, after the middle of the sixteenth century, the heralds became more sophisticated and not only entered the scores into the cheques, but occasionally summarized the results in writing as was done for the tournament on November 5, 1559[28] where we read of the challengers and of the defenders (cf. illustration 8):

The chalengers—
The Lorde Robert Brake x[vj][16] staves and gave ij[2] attaints wherof one of the attaints was one the vissard: which is allowed for a staffe broken [curly bracket] x[vj] staves ij attaints.

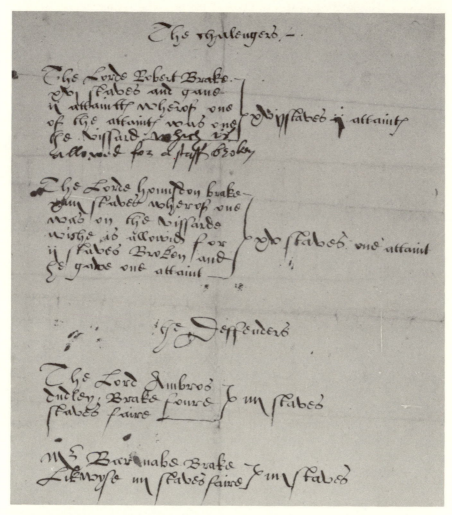

8. Summary of results for the tournament in Westminster, held on 5 November 1559. Taken from The College of Arms Mss, formerly Box 37, now in a portfolio. Copyright The College of Arms London, used by permission.

The Lorde Hounsdon brake x[14] staves wherof one was on the vissarde wiche is allowid for ij staves Broken and he gave one attaint [curly bracket] xv[15] staves one attaint.
The Deffenders
The Lord Ambros dudley Brake foure staves faire [curly bracket] iiij[4] staves
M[r] Barnabe Brake Likwyse iiij staves faire [curly bracket] iiij staves.[28] Cf. ill. 8.

In those days London citizens, order of preference, went to such tournaments first and foremost, and then, Midsummer Shows, Lord Mayors' Parades, and public executions.[29] Henry Machyn, a merchant-tailor and furnisher of funerals, meticulously filled his diary with many details concerning the participants' attire, the kind of cloth worn, and colors. As a sort of undertaker, however, he was more interested in the latest funeral-fashions than in the tournaments themselves. Of the tournament in question he writes:

The v day of November ther was grett justes at the quen['s] palles, and ther was my lord Robart Dudley and my lord of Hunsdon, wher the chalengers, and all they wher [in] skarffes of whyt and blake, boyth the haroldes and trumpeters and the fotmen with skarffes of red and yelow sarsenett . . .
The vi day was bered in sant Androse in Holborn master Mortun sqwyre, with a harold of armes, a pennon of armes, and a cott armur, with a dozen of skochyons.[30]

Machyn's main interest, of course, was the fashion at burials and funerals. The funerals of that period were staged with chivalrous splendor, coats of arms, pennants, and heralds. As we have seen, Machyn attended a funeral just one day after the tournament. When we compare the entries in his diary with the details in the heralds' cheques and the summary of scores, we get an idea of the historical value of genuine score-cheques. Such cheques supply authentic evidence because the judges' and the scoring heralds' positions were very close to the tilt. This is reported by Henry Machyn concerning a joust held on April 28, 1560, when a judge was hit by a piece of a broken lance:

. . . and ther stod in the standing as juges my lord markes of Northamtun, my lord of Ruttland, and my lord of Penbroke, and my lord admerall and the Frenche inbassadur, and master Garter and master Norroy [two of the five chief heralds] dyd wrytt wome dyd rune; and by chanse of the brykyng of a stayff a pesse flew up wher the juges sitt and hyt my Lord Penbroke . . . The xxix day of Aprell whent to hanging ix men and one woman to Tyburne.[31]

Only one day after the tournament Machyn attended a public execution. Tournaments and executions, being Elizabethan spectacles, were well attended by the masses. Even if Machyn was not too explicit in regard to tournaments, he supplied evidence concerning the registration of the runs by the heralds and the position of the judges near the scene of action.

That the method of scoring had to be brought back to mind is clearly seen by a marginal note on a cheque-list for a tilting at the barriers staged on May 7, 8, 1571. [32] Here a senior herald, in the most illegible scrawl by a contemporary hand imaginable explained to an inexperienced junior (cf. illustration 9):

/ and in these
iij lynes there is marked in the
uppermost the taints in the
myddle the Spaires broken
and in the lowest
Spayrs disalowed /
and in the long lynne

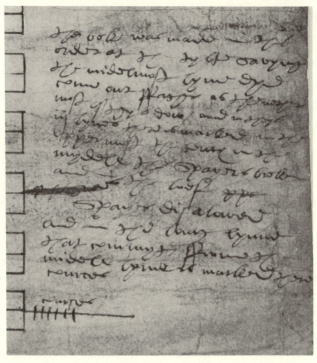

9. A marginal note explaining the method of scoring on a cheque-list for a tilting at
the barriers, held on 7/8 May 1571. Taken from The College of Arms Mss (cf. ill. no.
8). Copyright The College of Arms London, used by permission.

that commyth ffrome the
middle lynne is marked their
courses.[32]

At the Accession Day Tournament held on November 17, 1588, which also
featured as "the climax of the festivities to celebrate the defeat of the Spanish
Armada," [33] the heralds applied a different method for scoring (cf. illlustration
10). As a cheque-list for this event clearly shows, they used pins and pricked
the scores.[34] There are pinpricks for lances broken on the body on the top line
and for charges run on the extension of the middle line. Pinpricks are real holes
in the manuscript.

Exactly the same pinprick method was used in a surviving cheque-list for the
Accession Day Tournament held on November 17, 1589 which is shown in
illustration 11.[35] This proves that pinpricking was fairly common in those days.

When the twenty-eight-year-old earl of Essex was the only challenger of fifteen
answerers for the Accession Day Tournament on November 19, 1594 (cf. illustration 12), he rode six charges against each of them, breaking fifty-seven lances

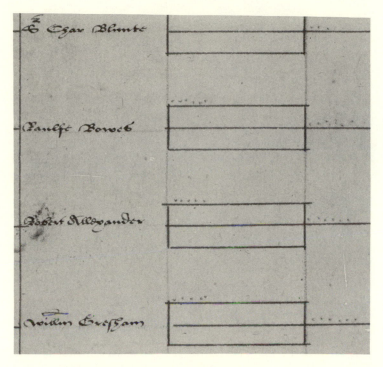

10. A pin-pricked cheque-list of the Accession Day Tournament, held on 17 November 1588. Enlarged section. Taken from The College of Arms Mss (cf. ill. no.8) Copyright The College of Arms London, used by permission.

in honor of Queen Elizabeth.[36] The number of charges is no longer marked because it was always the same. However, the lances broken by Essex are pinpricked above the middle line. When meeting the earl of Sussex, Essex scored two lances broken on the head.

After having acted as the queen's champion tilter for thirty years, Sir Henry Lee, "being now by age ouertaken,"[37] resigned his post at the end of the Accession Day Tournament on November 17, 1590. At the top of the cheque-list [38] for that day we find the entry "vj courses"- "Juste at Westms 17. november 1590" (cf. illustration 13). For the last time Sir Henry Lee's name appears at the head of a list of twenty-six knights who were grouped into thirteen pairs to run against each other.[39] As on the Accession Day Tournaments of the preceding years, the number of charges run is no longer expressly marked on the extension of the middle line. The standard was six charges. The scores for November 17, 1590 are entered on the top line of the individual cheques with pen and ink. After Lee had resigned, the new champion tilter, the earl of Cumberland, Lord Strange, and the earl of Essex issued a challenge against all comers for November 19, 1590. The scores for two of these three challengers for November 19 are

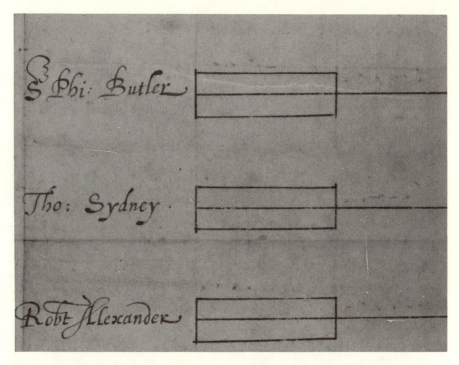

11. A pin-pricked cheque-list of the Accession Day Tournament, held on 17 November 1589. Enlarged section. Taken from The College of Arms Mss (cf. ill. no.8). Copyright The College of Arms London, used by permission.

pinpricked above their names. They read: "These vij [sets of] courses the erl of cumberland dyd Run and brake every staffe which is in all xlij." Seven lines of charges are indicated (cf. illustration 14), and when we count the pinpricks, their number is exactly 42. On the left-hand side we find six rows of pinpricks above the name of Lord Strange (cf. illustration 15). The text on the left margin reads:

These xxxj [courses] the
lord Strange dyd
Course as a challenger
on thursday the
xix of november
the year abouvesayd
he ran vj [sets of] courses
with vj severall
gentellmen.

There are five blanks in the six rows of pinpricks, and when we count the pinpricks their number is exactly thirty-one. Unfortunately, there is a triangular

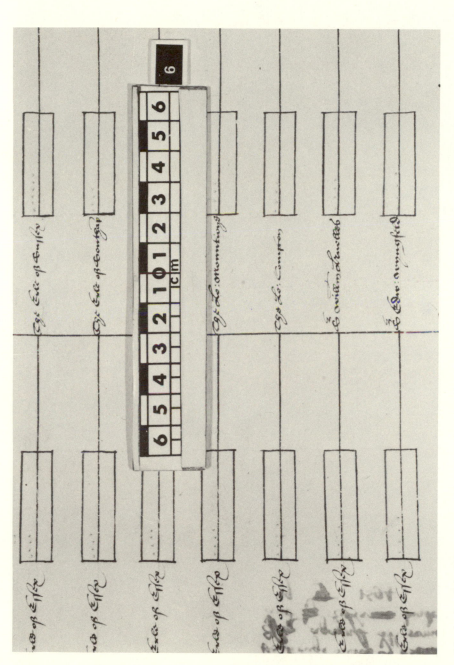

12. A pin-pricked cheque-list of the Accession Day Tournament, held on 19 November 1594. Enlarged section. Taken from The College of Arms Mss (cf. ill. no.8). Copyright The College of Arms London, used by permission.

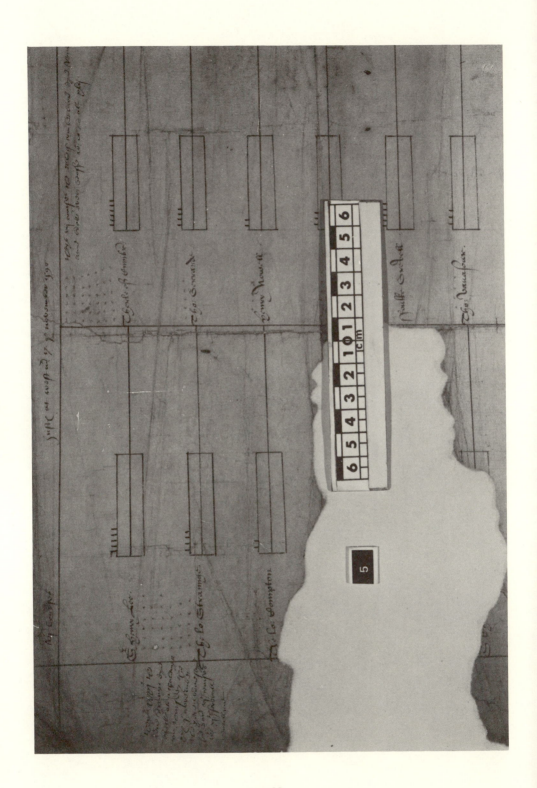

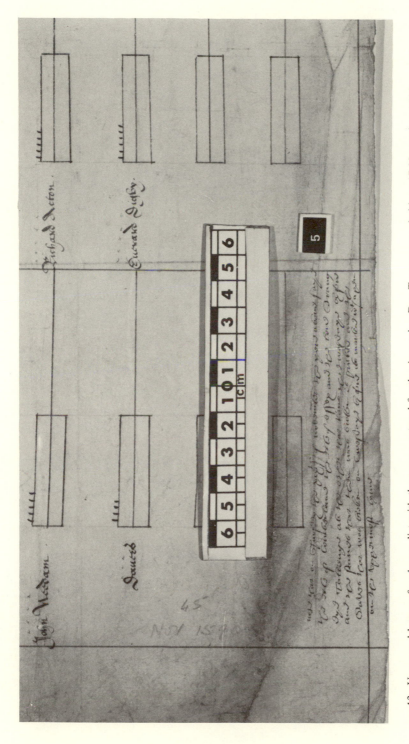

13. Upper and lower of a cheque-list with the scores entered for the Accession Day Tournament, held on 17 November 1590 and pin-pricked scores for 19 November 1590. Taken from The College of Arms Mss (cf. ill. no.8). Copyright The College of Arms London, used by permission.

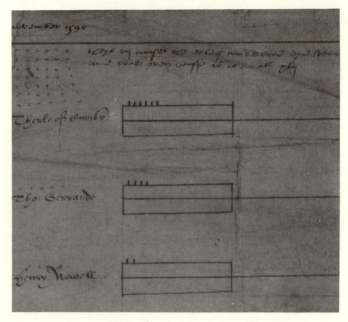

14. Pin-pricked section of the Earl of Cumberland's scores on 19 November 1590. Enlarged section of ill. no.13. Copyright The College of Arms London, used by permission.

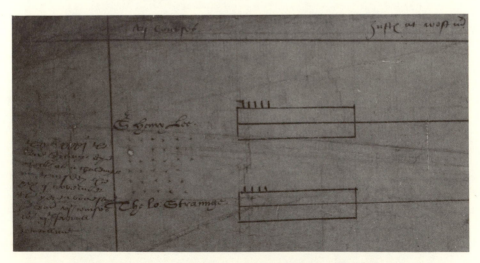

15. Pin-pricked section of Lord Strange's scores on 19 November 1590. Enlarged section of ill. no.13. Copyright The College of Arms London, used by permission.

16. A marginal note explaining the procedure of scoring for the Accession Day Tournament: staves broken on 17 November 1590 are entered by pen and ink, staves broken on 19 November are pin-pricked. Enlarged section of ill. no.13. Copyright The College of Arms London, used by permission.

hole in the cheque-list just where the earl of Essex's name (as the third challenger) must have been: in fifth position riding against "ffoulke Grevell" on the first day. That is why Essex's pinpricked score for the second day is lost forever. The fact that the heralds cleverly used the same cheque-list for two days is corroborated by a contemporary hand on the bottom of this list (cf. illustration 16). It reads:

note that on Thursdaye the xixth of november the yere abouv sayd the erle of Comberland the erle of essex and the lord Strang dyd challenge all the other that Rane the Twesdaye byfore and the staves that then was broken is pricked and the Staves that was broken on Twesdaye by fore is marked with a pen on the uppermost lynne.

In summary, we have seen that the heralds actually did the scoring, thus determining the best jouster. As far as the English tournament of the late fifteenth and sixteenth centuries is concerned, the legend that the prizes were awarded at the discretion of the ladies can be laid to rest. Such a function clearly belongs to the realm of medieval romantic fiction.

NOTES

1. *The Dictionary of National Biography*; see Lee, Sir Henry.

2. *The Works of George Peele*, ed. by Arthur H. Bullen (London: John C. Nimmo, 1888), II, p. 281.

3. Roy C. Strong, "Elizabethan Jousting Cheques in the Possession of the College of Arms II," *The Coat of Arms* (5, 34, 1958), p. 65.

4. On November 17, 1584, the queen herself presented the prizes; see Victor von Klarwill, *Queen Elizabeth and Some Foreigners*, trans. by T. H. Nash (London: John Lane, 1928), p. 332.

5. Harold Arthur, "On a MS. Collection of Ordinances of Chivalry of the fifteenth century, belonging to Lord Hastings," *Archaeologia* (2nd ser. VII, 1900), p. 40.

6. Arthur, "On a MS. Collection," p. 40.

7. Joachim K. Rühl, "Zur Leistungsquantifizierung im spätimittelalterlichen Turnier," *Brennpunkte der Sportwissenschaft*, ed. by Hans-Joachim Appell and Karl-Heinz Mauritz (St. Augustin: Academia Verlag Richarz, 2, 1988, 1), pp. 97–111.

Joachim K. Rühl, "Wesen und Bedeutung von Kampfansagen und Trefferzählskizzen für die Geschichte des spätmittelalterlichen Turniers," *Festschrift für Hajo Bernett: Sport zwischen Eigenständigkeit und Fremdbestimmung,* ed. by Giselher Spitzer and Dieter Schmidt (Bonn: Peter Wegener, 1986), pp. 86–112.

8. Lansdowne Ms. no 285; cf. Charles Ffoulkes. "Jousting Cheques of the Sixteenth Century," *Archaeolgia* (53, 1912), p. 32.

9. Cf. Sydney Anglo, *The Great Tournament Roll of Westminster* (Oxford: Clarendon Press, 1968), p. 47.

10. College of Arms Ms. M3, fol. 24b.

11. College of Arms Ms. M3, fol. 24b.

12. For a report of the heralds, see Francis Grose and Thomas Astle, *The Antiquarian Repertory* (London: Edward Jeffery, 1807–09), II, pp. 249–331. There is a smaller section in *The Great Chronicle of London,* ed. by Arthur H. Thomas and Isobel D. Thomley (London: G. W. Jones, 1938), pp. 312–315.

13. Anglo. *Tournament Roll,* p. 36.

14. Cf. Grose/Astle. *Antiquarian Repertory,* II, p. 297.

15. For November 17, 1584, we find: "Everyone who wishes to look on and have a seat on the stands must pay eighteen pence. As however one penny is of pure silver, it is worth as much as in our country [Germany] a groschen"; cf. von Klarwill, *Queen Elizabeth,* p. 331.

16. Von Klarwill, *Queen Elizabeth,* p. 331.

17. Grose/Astle, *Antiquarian Repertory,* II, p. 297.

18. Ibid.

19. Ibid., p. 299; cf. this line in the lower corner on the left-hand side of Exhibit 4.

20. Strangely enough, this fact is not mentioned in the herald's report.

21. Grose/Astle, *Antiquarian Repertory,* II, pp. 304–306.

22. Anglo, *Tournament Roll,* p. 39.

23. Grose/Astle, *Antiquarian Repertory,* II, pp. 306–307.

24. Ibid.

25. Anglo, *Tournament Roll,* p. 40.

26. Grose/Astle. *Antiquarian Repertory,* II, pp. 307–309.

27. Ibid., p. 311.

28. College of Arms Mss, formerly Box 37, now in a portfolio; tilt on November 5, 1559.

29. Public executions were not abolished until 1868.

30. *The Diary of Henry Machyn,* ed. by John G. Nichols (London: Camden Society 42; 1848), p. 216–17.

31. Ibid.

32. College of Arms Mss; cf. note 28. Tilt on May 7/8, 1571.

33. Strong, "Jousting Cheques," p. 65.

34. College of Arms Mss; cf. note 28. Tilt on November 17, 1588.

35. College of Arms Mss; cf. note 28. Tilt on November 17, 1589.

36. College of Arms Mss; cf. note 28. Tilt on November 19, 1594.

37. Bullen, *Works of Peele,* II, p. 282.

38. College of Arms Mss; cf. note 28. Tilt on November 17/19, 1590.

39. Bullen, *Works of Peele,* II, p. 286 gives a complete list of all the challengers and answers who competed on both days.

8

Sport in the Context of Non-European Cultural Tradition: The Example of Hawaii

GUNDOLF KRÜGER

POINT OF DEPARTURE: THE EMIC-ETIC DICHOTOMY

Because of the historical and cultural relativity of the term *sport*[1] it is impossible to effect a cross-cultural transfer of the values implied in the modern concept of sport. Examination of old ethnographic field reports reveals that there are two quite separate and contradictory approaches to the subject of sport and games.

The majority of these reports recognize sport in non-European societies as a distinctive cultural manifestation, but frequently place sport and games in the same category as the so-called fine arts. In these reports, sport is considered a physical expression of pleasure, recreation, or joy, and is equated taxonomically with music, dancing, poetry, and painting. Categories such as the elements of competition or achievement have no place in this picture.

A small minority of field reports strictly avoid the term *sport* in the context of non-European societies. Although these works do mention physical exercises which in terms both of organization and course of events correspond to what we would call sport, they are at best "the so-called gymnastic exercises of primitive peoples."[2] This fear of misinterpreting the term *sport* as seen in a cross-cultural context may be traced to its alleged "deep roots in ritual,"[3] an opinion still widely held today. According to this thesis, we may speak of sport only in connection with the non-European societies that, having renounced their traditional religions, have assimilated with European industrial societies. On the other hand, those who support the sport-as-ritual thesis are hard pressed to find any original historical evidence for their position earlier than the eighteenth century, the time of the first great explorations. Because the great majority of so-called primitive peoples used only spoken language, hardly any adequate written records exist which can help unravel the question of origin. We might therefore just as well argue from the opposite position and maintain that the process of secularization did not necessarily apply to a phenomenon that was originally religious in nature, but that "early forms of sport, though overlaid with religious significance, were in essence composed of elements of games-playing, gymnastics and competition."[4]

As we turn to the example of the traditional society of Hawaii, we find that "sport" cannot be examined adequately by using terms borrowed from the fine arts. Nor can historical connections be derived from the field of religion or religious ritual.

Records available since James Cook's discovery of Hawaii in 1778 provide no confirmation for the ritual thesis in the case of the preindustrial form of society under consideration. Although gymnastic-type exercises were practiced during religious ceremonies, it must remain an open question as to whether these exercises, which in our society would earn the name of sport, would have been so regarded by the protagonists and spectators themselves. On the other hand, the earliest written sources of indigenous Hawaiians do contain expressions involving exercises that are regarded as sport and games in the European sense. The word *pa'ani* covers everything connected with sport and games in the widest sense, from running and dicing to juggling and ball games.[5] The word *hakaka le 'ale 'a* narrows the perspective down to "competitive sports" and covers exercises like fistfighting, wrestling, bowling, javelin throwing, and surfing.[6] Aside from their frequently ritualistic patterns of movement, these exercises are nowhere explicitly described as a cult or a form of religious expression. We are therefore left with an incomplete evaluation in terms of the theoretical requirements of modern cognitive anthropology.

Few of the early European eyewitnesses at the turn of the nineteenth century managed to integrate themselves into the strange culture of the geographically isolated island world of Hawaii. Because of language barriers and misunderstandings produced by too short a period of contact, perceptions and judgments have tended to be narrow and European-biased. As a result a proper emic perspective has not been approached. The existence of intrinsic motivations that could help explain whether the exercises served a cathartic or religious purpose or a ritualistic or ascetic purpose, or whether, on the other hand, they were practiced in the spirit of *'l'art pour l'art'* (purely autotelic motives) is not clear from the primarily European source materials available. In short, we do not possess any fully differentiated indigenous set of terms relating to "sport" in Hawaii.

The researcher concerned with sources and records is therefore reduced to an etic perspective. The only viable approach to the meaning and function of traditional Hawaiian physical culture has to be based on the modern or contemporary concept of "sport" with its own system of reference and taxonomies.

"SPORT": SYSTEM OF REFERENCE AND PARTICULAR CATEGORIES

Unlike *sport,* the term *achievement* is by no means the exclusive property of the Western world. Achievement, which may be defined as activity or behavior aimed at a given standard of excellence, is closely bound up with such terms as *competition* and is an anthropological constant. "Behaviour of this kind has taken place in all cultures and epochs. Every society known to us possesses norms sanctioning behaviour as positive or negative. Every society approves and disapproves."[7] The standards set for achievement, however, vary from society to society, which gives the term a varying set of values, ranging from the all-embracing one found in so-called achievement-oriented societies (*Leistungsgesellschaften*) down to sets of rules that canalize the behavior of members of a given society or are no longer accepted by them.

In the same way, the notion of achievement in sport varies from society to society. We may therefore look at Hawaiian physical culture in terms of its agonal characteristics, which permit those forms of behavior that conform to the residual categories of physical activity, nonproductivity, and social activity[8] to be called sport. In other words, sport is the term applied to all Hawaiian physical exercises in which the motor activities of the body explicitly possess the following basic characteristics: (1) they are practiced; (2) they can be improved by training; and (3) they are potentially competitive. The exercises must also be unconnected with everyday activities (e.g., fishing, hunting, or transportation) or with military training or actual war.

Based on these premises then, we have the following groupings for Hawaiian physical exercises:[9]

1. *Combatant Sports Activities*
   Boxing: *moko moko*
   Wrestling
   hakoko
   Variations on *hakoko*
   ku'i-a-lua
   Fencing with rods: *kaka la'au*

2. *Heavy Athletic Activities*
   Trials of strength under the heading "Pressing"
   Trials of strength under the heading "Pulling"
   Trials of strength under the heading "Lifting"

3. *Hunting Sports Activities*
   Deep sea fishing: *aku*
   Archery: *pana'iole*

4. *Throwing and Rolling Activities*
   Throwing (overarm)

Javelin: *'o 'o ihe*
Variations
Throwing (underarm)
Javelin or club throwing: *pahe 'e*
Variations
Bowling: *'ulu maika*

5. *"Racing"*: *hei-hei*
Running
hei-hei kukini
Variations
Sledging: *he 'e holua* (including variations)
Swimming
hei-hei 'au
Variations or complementary exercises
Rowing: *hei-hei wa 'a*
Surfing: *he 'e nalu*

Following the approach taken by Eichberg (1978)[10] and the expanded concept of Guttmann (1979)[11] relating to cross-cultural comparisons in sport, we can now employ the following assessment criteria, with appropriate modifications, for the physical culture of Hawaii:

• Rules for sports competitions (during course of play, etc.).
• Objective rating of competitions (result of competition, etc.).
• Forms of quantifying sports performances.
• Guarantees of success and professionalization tendencies.
• Level of secularization.

THE TRADITIONAL SPORTS ACTIVITIES OF HAWAII: BASIC TENDENCIES

The exercises that could be described as "national sports" were characterized by high spectator interest and by the competitive participation of all sectors of society, regardless of social position, age, or sex. They included boxing (*moko moko,*) throwing (underarm), bowling (*'ulu maika*), and surfriding (*he 'e nalu*). The oral traditions reveal a high rate of female participation in competitions, particularly in surfing.[12] Swimming, diving, and high-diving were also extremely popular pastimes, but documentation in terms of competitive sport is too scanty to permit them to be described as popular sports.

Three exercises were the province of the privileged classes, the *ali 'i*, especially the tribal chiefs. Together with Thorstein Veblen, we can treat these as typical examples of the idle pastimes of a small but powerful group of the economically elite, sanctioned by the feudal rules of the society in which they lived. One of them was sledging (*he 'e holua*) on beautifully laid-out summer tracks several hundred meters in length; this land was the exclusive property of the tribal chiefs. The other two pastimes were deep sea fishing (*aku*) and archery (*pana 'iole*), the only forms of hunting known in Hawaii. The bow and arrow were used exclusively in competitive sports, never as weapons of war or in food acquisition.[13]

For the most part, however, the exercises were closely connected with military training and fitness. "Warlike games" were a definite part of the physical training of the chieftains' sons and of their corps of guards. Women had no place here. Included in this group are all the combatant sports—except boxing—all heavy athletics, and the throwing sports (overarm) like *o' 'o ihe*. The combatant sport of fencing with rods (*kakala 'au*) was not, as one might suppose, borrowed from the martial arts; rather it was part of training for spear-handling.[17] Thus fencing with rods was used for military training purposes, but never in war itself.

The Hawaiians, as all early European sources unanimously agree, were outstanding at aquatic sports. No other country in the world in pre-European history developed surfing (*he 'e nalu*) to as high a degree as Hawaii.[15] Only in Hawaii do we have a record of its technically most difficult form: standing upright on the surfboard, together with different types of board construction adapted to varying surf conditions.[16]

BODILY AWARENESS, THE COMPETITIVE MENTALITY, AND BETTING

"Keeping fit in mind and body" in their leisure time was of central importance for Hawaiians.[17] "Health and vitality (*ola*), comeliness, and strength (*u 'i*) were qualities of the whole body (*Kimo*) that were carefully fostered."[18] The environment, of course, helped promote this attitude.

As Mitchell (1972) shows, the vegetable and animal sources of nourishment were quite sufficient to cover the Hawaiian's daily needs of carbohydrates, proteins, vitamins, minerals, and trace elements, as measured by today's standards.[19] Food was carefully cooked in clay ovens, and as a result vital constituents were largely preserved. The processing of taro for flour left behind a kind of alkaloid starch that compensated for the rather low supply of vitamins in fruits; and it kept for several weeks in a fermented state.[20] Herbs were made of edible marine plants and provided calcium. *Opihi,* limpets growing on the rocks, contained a high proportion of Vitamin A. Fish was rich in protein and provided Vitamin D. Continuous exposure of the skin to the sun's ultraviolet rays aided this process. A good nutritional foundation was a major reason for the Hawaiians' freedom from infectious diseases. Their teeth and hair remained healthy and intact to an advanced age. The men reached an average height of 180 centimeters with a "strikingly muscular physique."[21] Their attainment of an athletic physique, together with the preservation of health, was a characteristic sign of the Hawaiians' bodily awareness. Their ideal of the body finds expression in numerous petroglyphs. Drawings made by early European visitors show Hawaiians as conforming anthropologically to the Grecian ideal: the facial expression, physique, and posture of athletes show strong resemblances to ancient models.[22]

Hawaiian athletes were looked after by professional healers called *Kahuna lo milomi* and *Kahuna lua*. There were a total of fifteen such medical groups set up by specialization. Not only were these healers trained in medicine, but they also played roles as trainers and physical educators. The *Kahuna lo milomi* possessed specialized knowledge and experience in massage. They knew "just how to manipulate and massage and pound sore and stiff muscles, and to bring relief"; the *Kahuna lua,* as boxing and wrestling instructors, knew "how to tie up the muscles of an antagonist, and the secrets of releasing the incapacitated muscle, which made Hawaiian wrestling so skilled."[23] Like Japanese *ju jutsu,* the Hawaiian wrestling technique was based on the esoteric knowledge of the *kahuna lua*: "The kahuna adept at lua had a knowledge of anatomy, especially nerve and muscle centers. He also believed that the stomach was the basis of strength, shrine of good health and seat of learning."[24]

In addition, a group of trainers, of whom no further description exists, were exclusively responsible for "sports training" (*kai* or *kahee*)[25] and physical education, including that of younger sons of chieftains.

Individualism and the encouragement of a competitive mentality occupy a remarkably prominent position. The "typical children's games" described by Bryan (1938)[26] primarily involved exercises that emphasized individual performance and were competitive in nature. The element of individual competition was also clearly dominant in the sports contests of the *moho,*[27] who were regarded as highly trained specialists in particular disciplines. There were no team competitions apart from tug-of-war, rowing, and a bloodless form of fencing with blunt spears.[28] This concept of competition is stressed by the term *ho 'o papa,* which in its literal translation means "to come into particularly hard contact with one another." In its wider meaning it stands for the principle of man-to-man competition, especially mental, challenging a person with knowledge of all the answers.[29] *Ho 'o papa* was a form of "constructive element of mental aggression,"[30] first, in the training of logic, intellectual abilities, eloquence and memory, and second in the field of physical education. In the present case, that of sports competition, *no 'o papa* was a ritualized challenge to an increased level of physical commitment.

Events always followed the same format. Before a match each competitor would make a show of disparaging the other's abilities and would touch the other in order to feel out weak spots in his physique. This mutual disparagement would be heightened by insults from the rival groups of supporters in the audience. The words "Go and eat chicken dung"[31] signified the call to battle. Kamakau gives the following formal expression for this challenge procedure: *ike ina aouli oka 'ano ona kanaka* (briefly, "to size up a man").[32]

In connection with this competitive mentality another tendency can be found in a cruder form in Hawaii than in any other Polynesian island, namely, betting (*pili wai wai*).[33] According to Malo, betting pure and simple provides the basic attraction for sports competition in Hawaii.[34] The foundations of sports like rowing were originally based on gambling: "The ancient Hawaiians were very fond of betting on a canoe race. When they wished to indulge this passion, people selected a strong crew of men to pull their racing canoes." Ii lists the sports which to his recollection attracted the most wagering at the turn of the nineteenth century: running, rowing, boxing, wrestling, and surfing.

Organized tournaments of these sports were attended by up to 10,000 spectators in the arenas (kahua).[36] Men and women of all ages and strata of society took part in betting. Stakes ranged from everyday objects like garments or food to a person's total possessions. On one occasion the attention of James Cook's sailors was attracted to the enraged behavior of a man who had bet on a race and lost three knives with iron blades that he had just exchanged for half his worldly goods with the Europeans.[37] When a particular competitor lost, his supporters would actually fight with the victorious side.[38] Betting became a social evil during the first phase of European contact: spectators wagered away their bodies and their personal freedom.[39] This most unpleasant form of betting was called pili iwi—"wagering away one's body." People would put themselves up as stakes and if they lost they would be enslaved by the victor.[40] Malo makes clear (and this is reinforced by a myth from pre-European times cited by Kamakau[41] that "wagering away one's body" had nothing to do with European influence but was already entrenched in the traditional betting culture. Only with the arrival of the Europeans, however, did betting take on such excessive forms that the first King of Hawaii, Kamehameha I, put a legal stop to it at the beginning of the nineteenth century.

THE CHIEFTAIN'S CORPS OF GUARDS: INSTITUTIONALIZED ATHLETES

Oral traditions refer to a large number of bloody battles fought in the seventeenth and eighteenth centuries between chieftains of different islands in the Archipelago. The main causes were:

1. A population increase.
2. The increased power of priests, who demanded the building of bigger temples and more sacrificial victims.
3. Disputes between related chieftains over title to land, mainly in consequence of inheritance.
4. Aristocratic "pastimes"[42] and "love of man-to-man combat,"[43] the chance to win prestige being an important factor here.

Although young ali 'i had always had enough leisure time owing to their aristocratic privileges to indulge in sports competitions, new military developments in Hawaii led to the formation of an independent social group. The best competitive sportsmen began to be recruited from this group and became the chieftain's corps of guards. Composed of leading specialists from individual disciplines (*moho*), they were separated into groups of warriors, messengers, and bodyguards. They underwant physical training daily for which they received regular wages paid out of the tribute collected by their chieftains. For this reason they can be described as a professional organization.

Professional soldiers in the sense of a standing army did not exist in the traditional culture, as Ellis[44] and Alexander[45] stress. Not until the first phase of European contact before the arrival of the missionaries in 1820 did a move take place away from "warlike specialists"[46] toward the formation of regular military units.

The guards were mainly of common stock and through their positions often enabled their families to improve their own lot in society. The worthiest and most successful competitors and warriors among them, like trainers and instructors in similar positions, were able to rise socially into the class of the *al'i 'i* and to lay the basis through well-planned marriages for the continued social advancement of their branch of the family.[47]

Although the group of warriors known as *koa* were trained mainly in wrestling, boxing, javelin throwing, fencing, and heavy athletics, the training of messengers (*kukini*) consisted of track and breathing exercises together with short pace-change and long-distance running. All *kukini* were subjected to strict dietary regulations.[48]

Men of outstanding physical strength were employed as bodyguards. They were experts in a type of self-defense known as *lua* which was kept secret from the common people. As sports contests, *lua* events always took place in the inner circle of the chief and his relatives. The public was excluded.[49] After the regency of Kamehameha I, the *lua* experts were joined by a second group of bodyguards, the spear-throwers (*keiki 'o 'o ihe*).[50] Since the spear was considered to be a life symbol, the spear-throwers were supposed to symbolize future peace. It remains an open question whether this group of bodyguards was called into existence under direct European influence at the end of the eighteenth century or whether they were the result of the internal policies of Kamehameha I.

In addition to training in war, an important aspect behind the all-round athletic training of the chieftains' corps of guards described above was preparation for an annual series of sports events that lasted four months. Wars were prohibited during this festival, known as *makahiki*. The best competitors made appearances there—in particular those from the semiprofessional guards' group—and represented their tribal chiefs in the "all-island-championships."

THE MAKAHIKI FESTIVAL

According to the creation myth of Hawaii, the wife of the god *lono,* one of the three highest ranking gods in Hawaiian mythology, disappeared one day at the end of a long journey during the changing season between summer and winter. In the course of his subsequent vain searches for his wife, *lono* became involved in a large number of sports contests on all the Hawaiian islands.[51] Every year he took up the search for her anew. His regular appearances gave rise to his popular reputation as blessed creator of rain, and as guardian of the harvest and the ritual thanksgivings associated with this role, which found final expression in the tradition of the organized makahiki festival series. This festival began after the disappearance of the Pleiades in autumn, which heralded the end of harvest, and lasted until the end of January. Both the Hawaiian calendar and counting system take account of the official character of this festival. In the traditional culture, the lunar year provided the basis of reckoning for these festivals. Lunation produced a synodic month, which consisted of only twenty-nine and a half days. The remaining half day was probably included alternately with the last day of the old month or the first day of the new one.

Altogether this corresponded to a three-phase view of the month: $3 \times 10 = 30$. This ten-day unit based on the lunar cycle then provided the foundation for the Hawaiian decimal system, or *anahulu*. In addition, the number 10 possessed symbolic significance: it appears frequently in poems and songs, and it forms the basis of calculation that was later used as the foundation for the scoring system in sports competitions. (The winner was the first person to reach 10 points.[52]) The Hawaiians were aware of the existence of the solar year as well as the 360-day lunar year, and accordingly dedicated five days in honor of the symbolic appearance of *lono*. These days represented the religious core of the festival. Following a series of ritual renewal procedures and processions through all parts of the islands, all geographical boundaries in the archipelago and all social barriers were temporarily lifted. The festival was then given over to the profane activities of banqueting and sport.

As the "God of Sport" (*akua pa 'ani*),[53] *lono* was present at all contests symbolized by one of three holy wooden standards. Competitors asked him in temples especially erected for the championships for divine strength (*mana*) for victory.[54] On January 28, 1779, during the makahiki festival, James Cook and his men were the first Europeans to witness a traditional contest under the auspices of the god *lono*. It was a boxing match (*moko moko*):

We found a vast concourse of people assembled on a level spot of ground, at a little distance from our tents. A long space was left vacant in the midst of them, at the upper end of which sat the judges, under three standards,. . . . When the sports were ready to begin, the signal was given by the judges, and immediately two combatants appeared . . . (after having been invited into the ring by various gestures G. K.). Being advanced within reach of each other, they stood with both arms held out straight before their faces, at which part all their blows were aimed. They struck, in what appeared to our eyes an awkward manner, with a full swing of the arm; made no attempt to parry, but eluded their adversary's attack by an inclination of the body, or by retreating. The battle was quickly decided; for if either of them was knocked down, or even fell by accident, he was considered as vanquished, and the victor expressed his triumph by a variety of gestures. . . . He then waited for a second antagonist; and if again victorious, for a third, till he was, at last, in his turn, defeated. A singular rule observed in these combats is, that whilst any two are preparing to fight, a third person may step in, and choose either of them for his antagonist, when the other is obliged to withdraw. Sometimes three or four followed each other in this manner, before the match was settled. When the combat proved longer than usual, or appeared too unequal, one of the chiefs generally stepped in, and ended it by putting a stick between the combatants.[55]

These boxing matches were supervised by junior chieftains acting as referees.[56]

As already stated, boxing was the only type of combatant sport in which women were allowed to participate: "The women also have their boxing matches ... They however do not box under the same Etour moco moco as the men, it being necessary that theirs should be made especially for females, the men being taboo and the women being nore."[57] The opponents were required to stand up to one another frontally, and at arm's length, they were only allowed to aim for the face.[58] Remarkably, the combatants could punch only with the arm unbent, drawn back and swung forward, and could parry only with clenched fist and unbent arm. The normal type of defense with the bent forearm was not permitted. "The Hawaiians do not seem to have used the fore-arm, after the manner of modern practitioners of the 'noble art'. Each boxer sought to receive his opponent's blow with his own fist."[59] This technique, in which the combatants hit at one another with little or no defense, and which led to a rigid knockout, was used because the Hawaiians had failed to bring boxing to the fine art practiced on neighbouring islands.[60] They did not know any good method of parrying blows.

It is still uncertain whether punches were struck with the bare fist or with gloves. Culin[61] indicates that the boxers wrapped their wrists in *kapa*.[62] Other sources refer expressly to bare-fist fighting. The resulting injuries were mainly to the head and arms.[63] Opinions are divided as to the brutality of these boxing matches. Although Whitman[64] stresses that the fights took place in a relaxed, friendly atmosphere and that "the damage was seldom greater than a knockout or slight bruising," Malo delivers the following critical verdict: "The one who fell was often badly maimed, having an arm broken, an eye put out, or teeth knocked out. Great misery was caused by these boxing matches."[65] There are no eyewitness reports of fatalities; however, fights to the death reportedly did occur when enough was at stake. "These boxing matches often lead to wagers among the spectators, and not infrequently end in violence and death. At almost every shout from the ring, the natives of our household exclaim, Taha! taha mamuri make!—Ah, ah! By and by murder!—and inform us, that many are killed in the moku moku; and that only a few years ago forty men were murdered at one time, on the very spot now occupied by the exhibition."[66] Proper places existed not only for boxing but also for all other sports, in the form of official arenas, courses, or running tracks (*kahua*).

On the *kahua,* powers were vested in referees, who were recruited mainly from official ranks subordinate to the chiefs. Existing records do not reveal any evidence of interference in results by priests, or overriding powers exercised by high-ranking chiefs in the form of showing favor or disfavor with results. The contests were under the charge of adjutants, who could be chosen by the participants themselves. These, together with the spectators, could object to referees' decisions with which they disagreed.[67] Unfairly matched opponents were usually separated in preliminary rounds and then put into categories suitable to their abilities.[68]

The arena was marked out with spears, and competition tracks were given start and finish markers. In surfing competitions the start was called *kulana* and the finish *pua* (a buoy); in fixed-distance running races, both start (*pahuku*) and finish (*pahuhopu*) were marked by standards.[69] Results took the form of declarations of visual order of finish "first, second, third" (in the case of races), knockout decisions, and points scoring from 1 to 10.

Oral tradition tells of great performances by famous athletes, mostly in mythical or exaggerated form. As actual results measured in terms of time and distance, of course, these do not stand up to objective scrutiny. There are no proper records based on objective measurements made by letters, numbers, drawings, or symbols. A rough determination of records is possible through the basalt balls used not only for athletic balancing acts, but also for physical contests of the weightlifting type. These show astonishing similarities in shape and weight, but the Hawaiians have never regarded them as standard weights for the registration of records.[70]

Consideration of the course and organization of the makahiki festival gives a clear indication of its essential religious dichotomy, a dichotomy characteristic of Hawaii and of Polynesia as a whole.[71] Together with a symbolic renewal of ethnic identity, the festival provided a stable ritual to ensure a balance of power between the influence of the priests and the rule of the chiefs. Secularly organized sports contests in the chieftain's court followed the religious part of the festival according to a precise time schedule.[72]

SUMMARY

In the traditional culture of Hawaii the expression denoting achievement was *ho ó pāpā*. It was bound up with a competitive philosophy that was primarily individualistic. Nonteam events, combative or individual, were the predominant forms of sport. This firmly entrenched "idea of competition" is further emphasized by the Hawaiians' love of betting. The seriousness with which Hawaiians took physical fitness indicates that they leaned toward what we would today call a "cult of the body."

The corps of guards provided a recruiting ground for future outstanding athletes and sportsmen. These individuals specially trained in running, self-defense, javelin throwing and various other disciplines, can be described as semiprofessionals. They were paid out of revenues collected by their chiefs in the form of tribute. They received regular training from special teachers. In competitive events they were normally awarded prizes in kind.

The makahiki festival provided the official background for the "all-island championships." During this period, sports contests were conducted according to the strictest rules, ranging from accurately marked-out tracks and proper refereeing to a Hawaiian form of "seeding" of opponents.

The objective criteria for winning and losing employed by the Hawaiians (first to reach 10 points, knockout, first second, third, etc.) do not, on the other hand, enable any precise measurement of athletic achievement to be made in the sense of the modern record. There was no official system for handing down the top scores or performances. The organization of the championships was secular. A study of neither the festival nor its course yields any indication that these contests were originally based on religious cults. On the contrary, the nature of the various activities and movements involved point quite clearly to a connection with everyday work, military exercises, and favorable environmental conditions, for example, in aquatic sports.[73]

NOTES

1. This chapter represents a summary of the findings of Gundolf Krüger, "Sportlicher Wettkampf auf Hawaii. Eine Konfiguration und ihr Wandel als Gegenstand ethnologischer Forschung," *Arbeiten aus dem Institut für Völkerkunde der Universität Göttingen 21* (Göttingen, 1986). On the historical relativity of sport, see, for example, Henning Eichberg, "Mass und Messen in der frühen Neuzeit. Der Sport als Beispiel," in R. E. Vente (ed.), *Erfahrung und Erfahrungswissenschaft* (Stuttgart, 1973), pp. 128–141. Idem, "Leistung, Spannung, Geschwindigkeit. Sport und Tanz in gesellschaftlichem Wandel des 18./19. Jahrhunderts" (Stuttgart, 1978). On historical-cultural relativity, see Henning Eichberg, "Zur historisch-kulturellen Relativität des Leistens in Spiel und Sport," *Sportwissenschaft* 6, 1 (1976), pp. 9–34. Allen Guttmann, "Vom Ritual zum Rekord. Das Wesen des modernen Sport," *Reihe Sportwissenschaft 14* (Schorndorf, 1979).

2. Hans Damm, "Vom Wesen sogenannter Leibesübungen bei Naturvölkern. Ein Beitrag zur Genese des Sports," *Studium Generale* 13, 1 (1960). pp. 1–10.

3. For example, Carl Diem, *Weltgeschichte des Sports und der Leibeserziehung* (Stuttgart, 1960); W. Körbs, "Kultische Wurzel und frühe Entwicklung des Sports," *Studium Generale* 13, 1 (1960), pp. 11–21; Marie Luise Syring, "Das Kultische im Sport," *Du*, Juli (1976), pp. 10–15.

4. Hans Kamphausen, "Traditionelle Leibesübungen bei autochthonen Völkern. Ein problemorientierter Überblick," in Horst Ueberhorst (ed.), *Geschichte der Leibesübungen 1* (Berlin, 1972), pp. 64–109.

5. David Malo, "Hawaiian Antiquities," *Bernice P. Bishop Museum Bulletin, Spec. Publ. 2* (Honolulu 1898, repr. 1980); Samuel M. Kamakau, "Ka Po 'e Kahiko. The People of Old," *Bernice P. Bishop Museum Bulletin, Spec. Publ. 51* (Honolulu, 1964); John Papa Ji, "Fragments of Hawaiian History," *Bishop Museum Misc. Publ.* (Honolulu, 1959).

6. Kamakau, "Ka Po 'e Kahiko," p. 20.

7. Eichberg, "Zur historisch-Kulturellen," p. 11.

8. These constituent categories came from the contemporary German sociology of

sport: Detlef Grieswelle, *Sportsoziologie* (Stuttgart, 1978), pp. 28–35; G. Lüschen and K. Weis (ed.), "Die Soziologie des Sports," *Soziologische Texte 99* (Darmstadt, 1976), p. 9; Klaus Heinemann, "Einführung in die Soziologie des Sports," in Ommo Grupe (ed.), *Sport und Sportunterricht. Grundlagen für Studium, Ausbildung und Beruf, vol. 1* (Schorndorf, 1980), pp. 31–38.

9. Krüger, "Sportlicher Wettkampf auf Hawaii," pp. 58–97.

10. Eichberg, "Leistung," p. 213 f.

11. Guttmann, "Vom Ritual zum Rekord," pp. 1 ff.

12. Thomas G. Thrum, "Hawaiian Surfriding," *Hawaiian Almanac and Annual (1896)*, pp. 106–113; Martha Beckwith, "The Hawaiian Romance of Laieikawai," *Bureau of American Ethnology 33* (1919), pp. 285–666; David Kalakaua, "The Legends and Myths of Hawaii" (Tokyo, 1972; 1st ed., 1888); Abraham Fornander, "Fornander Collection of Hawaiian Antiquities and Folk-lore," *Memoirs of the B. P. Bishop Museum,* Vol. 4 (Honolulu 1916–1917), p. 510; W. D. Westervelt, " Legends of Old Honolulu" (London, 1915).

13. A. Ihle, "Der Bogen und seine Verwendung auf Tahiti," *Göttinger Völkerkundliche Studien 1* (1939), pp. 192–214; H. Plischke, "Bogen und Pfeil auf den Tonga-Inseln und in Polynesien," *Göttinger Völkerkundliche Studien 2* (1957), pp. 207–25. Donald D. K. Mitchell, "Hawaiian Warfare and Weapons," *Bishop Museum—Manuscripts MSC2* (Honolulu, 1976), p. 14.

14. "Charles W. Kenn, "Japanese and Hawaiian Sports Similar," *Pan-Pacific Magazine 1* (1937), p. 29; Donald D. K. Mitchell, *Hawaiian Games for Today* (Honolulu, 1975), p. 36.

15. Ben Finney, "Surfboarding in Oceania—Its Pre-European Distribution," *Wiener Völkerkundliche Mitteilungen 2* (1959), pp. 23–36; idem, "Surfing in Ancient Hawaii," *The Journal of the Polynesian Society 68* (1959), pp. 327–47; idem, "Surfboarding in West Africa," *Wiener Völkerkundliche Mitteilungen 5* (1962), pp. 41–42; Ben Finney and James Houston, *Surfing. The Sport of Hawaiian Kings* (Tokyo, 1966).

16. Te Rangi Hiroa, *Arts and Crafts of Hawaii,* (Honolulu, 1964; 1st ed., 1957), p. 384. Dieter Schori, "Das Floss in Ozeanien. Formen, Funktion und Verbreitung des Flosses und flossartiger Schwimmkörper in der Südsee." *Völkerkundliche Beiträge zur Ozeanistik 1* (Göttingen, 1959), p. 151. Tahiti: see William Ellis, *Polynesian Researches,* Vol. 2 (London 1853), p. 224; Douglas L. Oliver, *Ancient Tahitian Society,* Vol. 1 (Honolulu, 1974), p. 315ff.

17. E. Damon, *Father Bond of Kohala. A Chronicle of Pioneer Life in Hawaii* (Honolulu, 1927), p. 114.

18. Craighill Handy and Mary K. Pukui, *The Polynesian Family System in Ka-u, Hawaii* (Wellington, 1958), p. 92.

19. Donald D. K. Mitchell, *Resource Units in Hawaiian Culture* (Honolulu, 1972), pp. 169–99.

20. John H. Wise, "Food and Its Preparation," in C. Handy and K. P. Emory (eds.), *Ancient Hawaiian Civilization* (Honolulu, 1965), pp. 95–104.

21. Mitchell, *Resource Units in Hawaiian Culture*, p. 191.

22. Johanna Agthe, "Die Abbildungen in Reiseberichten aus Ozeanien als Quellen für die Völkerkunde (16–18. Jahrhundert)," *Arbeiten aus dem Institut für Völkerkunde der Universität Göttingen 2* (Göttingen, 1969), pp. 169, 175, 189.

23. John H. Wise and Nils P. Larsen, "Medicine," in Handy and Emory (eds.), *Ancient Hawaiian Civilization,* pp. 257–67.

24. James T. Fitzpatrick, "The Ancient Art of the Bodyguards of Hawaiian Kings," *Black Belt Magazine* 4, 11 (1966), p. 21.

25. Malo, "Hawaiian Antiquities," p. 219.

26. E. H. Bryan, "Ancient Hawaiian Life" (Honolulu, 1938), p. 51; for example dart throwing, juggling, knot tying, jumping from high places into pools, diving.

27. Kamakau, "Ka Po 'e Kahiko," p. 20.

28. Ji, "Fragments of Hawaiian History," pp. 63, 67; Stewart Culin, "Hawaiian Games," *American Anthropologist* 1, 2, (1899), p. 210 f; Malo, "Hawaiian Antiquities," p. 222; Richard Karutz, "Die Spiele der Hawaiier," *Globus 76* (1899), p. 341; Jurij F. Lisjanskij, *A Voyage Round the World in the Years 1803–1806* (London, 1814), p. 119; Otto v. Kotzebue, *Entdeckungsreise in die Südsee und nach der Beringstrasse . . . unternommen in den Jahren 1815, 1816, 1817 und 1818 . . . auf dem Schiffe Rurick*, Vol. 2 (Weimar, 1821), p. 34.

29. Martha Beckwith, "The Hawaiian Hoopapa," *American Anthropologist* 25, 4 (1923), p. 580.

30. Mary K. Pukui et al., *Mana I Ke Kumu (Look to the Source)*, Vol. 2 (Honolulu 1979), p. 218.

31. Malo, "Hawaiian Antiquities," p. 232; Abraham Fornander, "Relating to Amusements. Fornander Collection of Hawaiian Antiquities and Folk-Lore," *Memoirs of the B. P. Bishop Museum,* Vol. 6 (Honolulu, 1919–1920), p. 204.

32. Kamakau, "Ka Po 'e Kahiko," p. 20.

33. Fornander, "Relating to Amusements," p. 215, 217.

34. Malo, "Hawaiian Antiquities," p. 222.

35. Ji, "Fragments of Hawaiian History," p. 67.

36. W. D. Alexander, *A Brief History of the Hawaiian People* (New York, 1891), p. 88; C. S. Stewart, *Journal of a Residence in the Sandwich Islands During the Years 1823, 1824, and 1825* (London, 1970; 1st ed., 1830), p. 316; Robert Quinton, *The Strange Adventures of Captain Quinton* (New York, 1912), p. 460; John B. Whitman, *An Account of the Sandwich Islands* (ed. by J. D. Holt) (Honolulu, 1979), p. 55; Malo, "Hawaiian Antiquities," pp. 220, 225, 232.

37. James Cook, *A Voyage to the Pacific Ocean*, Vol. 3 (London, 1784), p. 145.

38. Culin, "Hawaiian Games," p. 202.

39. Kenneth P. Emory, "Sports, Games and Amusements," in Handy and Emory (eds.), *Ancient Hawaiian Civilization,* p. 146.

40. Malo, "Hawaiian Antiquities," p. 226.

41. Kamakau, "Ka Po 'e Kahiko," p. 129.

42. Mitchell, "Hawaiian Warfare and Weapons," p. 1.

43. Pukui et al., "Mana I Ke Kumu," p. 212.

44. William Ellis, *Narrative of a Tour through Hawaii* (London, 1827), p. 133.

45. Alexander, *A Brief History of the Hawaiian People*, p. 31.

46. Thomas Bargatzky, "Die Rolle des Fremden beim Kulturwandel," *Hamburger Reihe zur Kultur- und Sprachwissenschaft,* Vol. 12 (Hamburg, 1978), p. 174.

47. Ibid., pp. 223–226; Mitchell, "Hawaiian Warfare and Weapons." p. 2; William Davenport, "The Hawaiian 'Cultural Revolution': Some Political and Economic Considerations," *American Anthropologist* 71 (1969), p. 5.

48. Malo, "Hawaiian Antiquities," p. 219; Ji, "Fragments of Hawaiian History," p. 67; Fornander, "Relating to Amusements," p. 198; Joseph Emerson, "Some of the

Old Hawaiian Games," *Bishop Museum NPS—Typescript/St. Case 4, Hms M 53 Misc.* (Honolulu, 1927), p. 1.

49. Malo, "Hawaiian Antiquities," p. 219; Fitzpatrick, "The Ancient Art of the Bodyguards," p. 20.

50. Kenn, "Japanese and Hawaiian Sports Similar," p. 24.

51. Ji, "Fragments of Hawaiian History," p. 72.

52. Malo, "Hawaiian Antiquities," p. 153.

53. Kamakau, "Ka Po 'e Kahiko," p. 20; Charles W. Kenn, "Ancient Hawaiian Sports and Pastimes," *Mid-Pacific-Magazine Oct.-Dec.* (1935), p. 308; Cook, *A Voyage to the Pacific Ocean,* p. 22ff; J. C. Beaglehole, *The Journals of Captain James Cook on His Voyages of Discovery,* Vol. 3, 1 (Cambridge, 1967), pl. 61; Malo, "Hawaiian Antiquities," p. 143ff; Ji, "Fragments of Hawaiian History," p. 71ff.

54. Emory, "Sports, Games and Amusements," p. 148; Te Rangi Hiroa, "Polynesian Religion," in Thomas Thrum (ed.), *Hawaiian Annual for 1933* (Honolulu, 1934), p. 64; Kalakaua, "The Legends and Myths of Hawaii," p. 40; Dorothy B. Barrere, "Hawaiian Aboriginal Culture," *Bishop Museum NPS-type-script 2* (Honolulu, 1961), pp. 107, 117.

55. Cook, *A Voyage to the Pacific Ocean,* p. 22ff.

56. Thomas Nickerson, "The Ancient Hawaiians Held Olympic Games." *Paradise of the Pacific* 48, 5 (1936), p. 23.

57. Whitman, *An Account of the Sandwich Islands,* p. 56.

58. Ibid., p. 56.

59. Malo, "Hawaiian Antiquities," p. 232.

60. In Beaglehole, *The Journals of Captain James Cook,* p. 627.

61. Culin, "Hawaiian Games," p. 207.

62. Cf. Karutz, "Die Spiele der Hawaiier," p. 341 and Quinton, "The Strange Adventures of Captain Quinton," p. 460. *Kapa* is beaten bark tissue. Cloths, mats, and clothing were produced from it.

63. Bryan, "Ancient Hawaiian Life," p. 48.

64. Whitman, *An Account of the Sandwich Islands,* p. 56.

65. Malo, "Hawaiian Antiquities," p. 232.

66. Stewart, "Journal of a Residence," p. 316.

67. Mary K. Pukui and Samuel H. Elbert, *English-Hawaiian Dictionary* (Honolulu, 1957); Mitchell, *Resource Units in Hawaiian Culture,* p. 129; Westervelt (1923), pp. 54–56; Kalakaua, "The Legends and Myths of Hawaii," p. 415ff.

68. For example, boxing: Cook, *A Voyage to the Pacific Ocean,* p. 22ff; surfing: Westervelt (1923), p. 57f.

69. Malo, "Hawaiian Antiquities," pp. 219, 223; Thrum, "Hawaiian Surfriding," p. 110; Westervelt (1923), p. 57; Culin, "Hawaiian Games," p. 210; Ji, "Fragments of Hawaiian History," p. 67.

70. Mitchell, "Hawaiian Games," p. 69; Wendell Clark Bennett, "Archaeology of Kauai," *Bernice P. Bishop Museum Bulletin 80* (1931), p. 78; Louis de Freycinet, "Voyage autour du monde . . . pendant les années" 1817–1820, 2, 2 (Paris, 1839; 1st ed., 1829), p. 606; Jacques Arago, *Narrative of a Voyage round the World . . . Commanded by Capt. Freycinet, during the years 1817–1820* (London, 1823), p. 131 f.

71. The Hawaiians always saw their activities as a whole as being dependent on a large number of hierarchically ranked gods. Just as every work process and every product had both its secular and sacred side, so was every festival and sports contest marked by

this worldly–religious dichotomy. See Craighill Handy, ''Religion and Education,'' in Handy and Emory (eds.), *Ancient Hawaiian Civilization*, pp. 47–61.

72. Malo, ''Hawaiian Antiquities,'' pp. 141–159.

73. This view is also held by Finney and Houston, ''Surfing,'' p. 53.

9

On the Limitations of Eichberg's and Mandell's Theory of Sports and Their Quantification in View of *Chikaraishi*

ARND KRÜGER AND AKIRA ITO

In a number of speculative essays, Henning Eichberg[1] and Richard D. Mandell[2] have tried to show that the attempt to quantify the output of physical performance is a typical trait of modern industrial society. They also maintain that it is relatively new[3] and specific to Western culture, and that, just as the word "record," it has spread particularly, from the 1880s onward with the rise of modern sport from Britain to the rest of the world. Because the two theses share some similarities, we will deal with both simultaneously, particularly since Mandell himself bases some of his theory on Eichberg.[4] Yet a certain amount of contradiction separates the two, especially concerning the notion of *industrial*. Whereas Eichberg includes the recorded performances of the philanthropists in his theory (one cannot speak of Germany being "industrial" at the turn of the nineteenth century), Mandell is far more narrow. Therefore, we will take issue particularly with Eichberg's theory as it includes most of Mandell's.

Eichberg randomly selected four sports as the basis for his study of secondary literature. As sole reasons for his selection of horse racing, foot racing (pedestrianism), boxing, and philanthropist athletics (athletic events organized to raise money for worthy causes) he mentions the availability of literature. As it turns out, his arbitrary choice of four out of more than fifty different sports is neither logical nor justified by historical criteria. If we were to deal with the question of recording and quantifying sports results, the sports to be selected would not include boxing. The reason is that in combative, one-against-one sports the length of a bout may be recorded for curiosity's sake, but it does not determine the winner directly. It would, however, include all other c-g-s (centimeters-grams-seconds) sports, such as swimming, weightlifting, archery, and throwing.

To clarify Eichberg's thesis that the change in European society in the late eighteenth century had its effect on social customs, archery would have been a far better sport to select. This sport began as shooting with bow and arrow for hunting purposes and as a military skill in the Middle Ages, became a game of luck and pompous festivity in the *Königsschiessen*[5] of the Renaissance, and in modern times became a sport of target shooting with numbered rings in which the distance from the center of the target was recorded. This development shows that the same physical act set in a different context of time and space does receive a different meaning.

Eichberg and Mandell as well could have avoided some of the ethnocentristic overtones of their theory. While archery has been practiced the world over, Eichberg and Mandell's limitations to sport that were typical only of Western Europe has led them to a wrong conclusion. At the time of the Industrial Revolution the British were at the height of Colonialism the world over, and so brought their sports with them. Thus, just as the British spread so did their sports.

Eichberg and Mandell's claim, however, goes further. According to Eichberg:

It is "natural," i.e., distributed among all men beyond the barriers of cultures or epochs, to jump and to run. But it is not "natural" in any way that running and jumping are done for the sake of quantifiable performances and that they are, indeed, measured.[6]

To verify or falsify such a far-reaching claim, it does not suffice to restrict oneself, as Eichberg did, to the Watusi high jumpers. A more logical and historical approach would have been more appropriate. The performance motive in Greek antiquity and in the Eighteenth Dynasty of ancient Egypt[7] reveals a certain amount of natural desire to win and to perform. Mandell believes that "the victory was *over* someone else and even a spectacular victory did not endure as an abstraction outside of the chronological time and geographical space in which it occurred. In other words, the victor lived in history; his performances did not."[8]

As Decker has shown, this notion is false. On the contrary, extraordinary performances have been recorded.[9]

Eichberg and Mandell did not use non-European sources, although an attempt to prove their point could have included research in other traditions of competitive sports. Japan, for example, has a long tradition of measuring and recording strength by *Chikaraishi*.[10] Records of rock lifting are extant all over the world and through all times, from Greek antiquity to modern Europe, where it had a special role in the Celtic tradition.[11] In all cultures there are myths of strong men who lifted and threw rocks.

The oldest dated *Chikaraishi* rock for lifting purposes is located at the Shinobu Shrine (1664), and the most modern date found is 1916 on a rock at the Setagaya-ku's Ohara Inari Shrine. For about 250 years *Chikaraishi* tested physical strength. The lifting and testing were most popular between 1830 and 1844. That is, it ended ten years before the United States forced the opening of ports for Western

Figure 9.1
Wooden Ranking Lists of _Banbuchi_

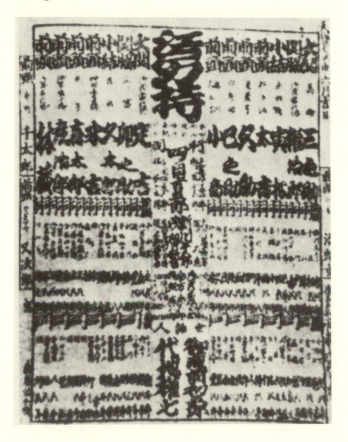

merchants and twenty-four years before the Japanese willingly adopted Western culture in the Meiji era. In the Edo period peasants and brewers of sake and soy sauce did their best to be men of muscle, for the strength of their arms determined their wages. They learned to move the _Chikaraishi_ and to lift the rock up step by step in order to increase their physical strength. Most of the _Chikaraishi_ that have been preserved are located in shrines, temples, and public halls on the Awaji Island. The majority of them were used for training rather than for competition, however. In the Tonami Region of the Toyama Prefecture, lifting _Chikaraishi_ is called _Banbuchi_ or _Banmochi_. Wooden ranking lists of _Banbuchi_ can be found in small shrines and temples of guardian deities in the villages of this region. Although the wooden ranking lists have been exposed to the weather, which makes it impossible to read the names, it is no doubt the ranking lists of the men taking part in _Banbuchi_ (Fig. 9.1).

The earliest ranking list that has been dated, "Men of Strength in Edo," is

Figure 9.2
Chikaraishi

from June 1836. Later lists have been dated April 1867 and October 1893. The measuring unit was *koku,* the standard rice bag. Practice *Chikaraishi* were usually 5 *koku* (90.195 liters) or 6 *koku* (108.234 liters) or 35 *Kan* (= 112 kg) (Fig. 9.2). However competitive performances of as much as 192 kg with one hand (see Figs. 9.3 and 9.4) have been recorded.

The performance and recording of strength events did not solely determine wages. Early in the Edo period castle towns developed, and post towns of major highways were well equipped. At that time young men from the farming villages, proud of their physical prowess, began to earn money by lifting up such things as straw rice bags, sake barrels, or big rocks at crossroads for the amusement of travelers. They would perform primarily during their leisure season when they were off farm work. Figure 9.5 shows two of these farmers performing their

Figure 9.3
Competitive *Chikaraishi* Performances

stunts. The picture is dated sometime between 1781 and 1789, in the middle of the Edo period. The poem in the picture explains that "men of strength cool themselves by the art of sweating." These public strength performances began around the middle of the Edo period and lasted until the beginning of the Meiji period.

During the same period Sumo wrestlers performed *Chikaraishi* in the intermission of their public matches to determine their strength. They were considered very entertaining. Rocks that have been used, as well as descriptions, have been preserved in the Hachiman Shrine in Ichigaya and the Setagaya in Tokyo. As the amusement quarters developed in the cities after the middle of the Edo period, street performers presented paid performances. They erected temporary tents so that they could show their stunts only to the paying public. Along with rope walking, acts of strength were performed. Even during the women's Sumo wrestling matches, lifting *Chikaraishi* and straw rice bags was included as an interlude. Not only the total strength, but also the way these heavy objects were handled was shown. When we look at the pamphlets that advertised Sannomiya Unosuke's *Chikaramochi* (strong men) performances (1836) at Edo, Asakusa, Osaka and Nanba, we find that all the stunts are still performed by acrobats today.

A *Chikaraishi* tradition also exists among fishermen and seamen. The *Chi-*

Figure 9.4
Close-up of One Hand Lift

karaishi at the Suizin Tsuchiura City Shrine was dedicated by the seamen of the Lake Kasumigaura sailing route, and the *Chikaraishi* at Choshi City (Hakuryu Gongen Shrine) was dedicated by the seamen who sailed from Edo. The many *Chikaraishi* now dedicated at Yokohama City Okamura Tenjin Shrine were used by the young local fishermen. The *Chikaraishi* left all over Osaka were used by the sailors of the Yodo River route and the dock workers (Fig. 9.6). The names of Edo Shinkawa Hichigoro and of Kanagawa Gonjiro are found on many *Chikaraishi* of the Edo and Yokohama area. Their names can also be found on the Edo *Chikaramochi* ranking list of 1867.

How did one get on a ranking list? The procedure was very similar to the one used today. The performance with graded *Chikaraishi* had to be presented in front of the central authorities of the respective shrine who judged and recorded

Figure 9.5
"Men of Strength Cool Themselves by the Art of Sweating"

them. The most famous strong men of the time took part in the lifting, as can
be seen not only from the repetition of the names on the ranking lists and on
other *Chikaraishi,* but also from pamphlets celebrating the performances of
certain *Chikaramochi* (e.g., Sannomiya Unosuke on the 1836 list).

Similar traditions of recording performances can likely be found in other non-
European cultures. What makes this Japanese example all the more valid is that
Japan did not open up to Western culture before 1868, having rigidly closed its
frontiers to all Western influence in 1639. The *Chikaraishi* tradition can therefore
be said to be purely Japanese.

This shows that the first point of the Eichberg/Mandell theory is false. The
attempt to perform and to have performances quantified and recorded did *not*
originate in Western Europe alone. Without doubt, however, the modern sports
brought over from Britain to the rest of the world did contain this element of

Figure 9.6
The *Chikaraishi* Tradition Among Seamen

competition and quantifiable performance. The first conclusion which can be drawn on the basis of the authors' hypothesis can therefore also be considered to be refuted. It is "natural" to jump, to run, and to lift weights, and for that matter it is also "natural" to record such performance and to prepare systematically for its improvement. It depends on the social setting of a society in time and space, however, whether or not such comparisons are desirable. The authors are correct when they state that physical activities have to be judged in their particular social context. They are wrong, however, to draw conclusions from a number of random samples without conducting any systematic research on the situation of sport as a whole.

Let us look at the other parts of their hypothesis and their explanations to determine how they hold up in the light of broader evidence. Eichberg claims that twelve stages are important for the change of emphasis from geometrical beauty of performance in the eighteenth century to recorded performance. With regard to rock lifting and rock putting (throwing), the class structure of the sport should not be overlooked. Whereas it takes a considerable degree of know-how that is available only from a certain educational level upward to measure most performances and a high degree of authority to make a ranking accepted, performances of pure strength have been primarily in use from a certain level downward. Even the rock lifting in the Celtic tradition (which was often char-

still served as preparation of the actual survival of the fittest. Yet in a competitive society the skills of competitive sport still serve well for survival. Yet other skills acquired there are equally helpful, such as the ability to concentrate at any given moment. In less competitive cultures where there are less competitive sports, the skills practiced in the sports world can be integrated into the real world.[68]

The "tuning in" or *ritual trance* has often been described as a characteristic of ritual.[69] Recent research, which resulted in the symposium *Shamans and Endorphins*, has shown that some of the earlier speculation about ritual trance has a sound biochemical foundation in neurobiology.[70] Two common symptoms of a trance can be found in many primitive rituals: (1) a state of detachment from the physical world, where the "possessed" seem to be occupied with an inner feeling of ecstasy or euphoria; and (2) a painfree state seen when the "possessed" is accepting acts that would normally result in considerable pain, like walking through fire or the piercing of the skin. Rhythmical, often strenuous, activity (frequently dancing) with some degree of monotony are often connected with ritual trance. At the end of the ritual those who have entered a trance often undergo a physical collapse. As has been described above, it is now certain that among the endogenous opioids and beta-endorphins in the brain, which can be measured as circulating beta-endorphins in the blood plasma, are responsible for this trance.[71] Opioids have an effect on the body only as it possesses receptors for the endogenous opioids. These have also been used to produce a ritual trance. The drug use of our time has been linked to the ritual of the technical age.[72]

But the sporting ritual has the same effect as the primitive and as exogenous opioids: Physical activity makes the beta-endorphin level rise; the concentration on the event can by itself create a trance. The endorphin level also rises under the many forms of stress. The high endorphin level allows a person to cope with stress which under different conditions is impossible to handle.[73] Rhythmical physical activities in sport or dance create an even higher endorphin level.[74] Primitive humans took doping substances with opioid content in ritual, just like athletes who could otherwise not reach their optimal performance. "Saturday night fever" and the jogging craze are modern forms of the ritual trance of modern Western society.

"The pivotal role of ritual in human adaptation is nowhere more evident than in societies under one form or another of stress."[75] Ecological stress may be defined as the feeling of being threatened to such an extent that the survival of all or most of the members of the society is at stake. This kind of stress should be kept apart from psychological stress, which results in synchronization. Seasonal changes may serve as an example of cyclical stress situations and epidemics for noncyclical ecological stress situations. In many societies many examples of rituals are connected with these changes. In the context of sport we may consider the rise of modern sport in the last third of the nineteenth century in industrial Britain as the result of just such noncyclical life-threatening stress situations. Relative overpopulation creates such ecological stress. The rise of sports to a true mass movement in post World War II Europe, the United States, and Japan coincides with the ecological threat of being destroyed by the bomb. Of course, we can also take medieval and early modern examples of sporting events in connection with the fair that took place at the beginning of the seasons. That is, rituals to solve cyclical crises. The football season brings order in the life of many and helps solve the cyclical stresses of the year.[76]

Just as the institution of authority deteriorates under severe and constant stress, so a traditional ritual may also lose its attraction as a response to crisis. Sports have often been quantified. Even societies that are considered noncompetitive have games and sports that quantify and thus cope with stress.[77] But the cult of a constant *citius-altius-fortius* is no longer a solution to the problems of modern Western societies which brought the world the modern sports movement as a ritual to cope with ecological stress. Just as the limits of sensible economic growth have become visible, so the limits of human performance without ergogenic aids is in sight. This has not yet led to deemphasizing the sports record, but noncompetitive sports are playing an increasingly important role in the leisure-time activity of the population. From there it is only a question of time until they will have reached a major public function. But even then the ritual function of all of modern sport for the individual's neuropsychological well-being remains.

In this discussion of ritual in sports, we have deliberately not included sports spectators, another topic which Allen Guttmann has dealt with.[78] The active participation of spectators is a regular feature of ritualized behavior.[79] It is interesting to note that rhythmical clapping and shouting can also cause a trance, that to appreciate the stress relieving effects of ritual, one does not have to take part on the floor. It is sufficient to be an involved witness.

CONCLUSION

We can now attempt to answer some of the initial questions about ritual in modern sport. Because of the sociobiological nature of ritual in modern sport, it is obvious that *ritual and record coexist side by side in modern society*. It is also obvious, that sport has always had a ritual function. There is no inherent difference between ancient and modern ritual in sports or elsewhere. Ritual fulfills a human need for structured communication to cope with stress and to prepare for the struggle for survival. We have attempted to give some explanation of the significance of sport as modern ritual. Not included are some of the fabulously conceptualized rituals of modern sports. Morever, there are better descriptions than the ones suggested here, as the cultural anthropology of play has come up with fascinating descriptions and interpretations of the ritual of modern sport.[80] We will not discuss them in the current context of the biosociological explanation of the ritual. Ritual in modern sport is a central theme that will serve well for interdisciplinary research combining the biological and the social sciences of sport.[81]

We should keep in mind, however, that unless we understand the brain function, we have no chance of understanding the deepest layer of the significance of ritual.[82] We can also conclude that, in the sociobiological sense of the interpretation, sports are never pursued for their own sake. We may not run in order to make the earth more fertile, but our running has a definite effect on the "external world, be it direct as in the case of metabolic regulation or indirect, as in the case of psychological (and neurophysiological) tuning."[83] Ritual in sports is an integral part of human evolution, necessary remains of a time when strenuous physical activity was a basic means of survival. As a biological function rituals exist side by side with the record, a cultural phenomenon.

NOTES

1. A. Guttmann, *From Ritual to Record. The Nature of Modern Sports*. New York: Columbia UP, 1978.

2. *Ibid.*, p. 26.

3. *Ibid.* p. 80.

4. M. Weber, *Wirtschaft und Gesellschaft. Grundriss einer verstehenden Soziologie.* Tübingen: Mohr, 1976 (5th ed.), pp. 321ff; p. 747. (Cf. *ibid.*, Köln: Kiepenheuer & Witsch 1964, p. 948.)

5. "In some passages, however, he uses formalism interchangeably with 'ritualism' which leads him to contradict himself because he says ritualism is incompatible with 'rational' law. In the context of pronouncements to this effect he uses 'formalism' or 'ritualism' to denote procedure where decisive weight is attached to gestures or the way in which a sentence is pronounced rather than to its content." S. Andreski, *Max Weber's Insights and Errors*. London: Routledge & Kegan Paul 1984, p. 88.

6. R. Collins, *Weberian Sociological Theory*. Cambridge, Mass.: Cambridge UP, 1986, p. 255.

7. B. S. Turner "The Rationalization of the Body. Reflections on Modernity and Discipline," in: S. Lash and S. Whimster (eds.), *Max Weber, Rationality and Modernity*, London: Allen & Unwin 1987, pp. 222–43.

8. H. Ueberhorst, "Ursprungstheorien," in *idem, Geschichte der Leibesübungen*, vol. 1, Berlin: Bartels & Wernitz, 1972, pp. 11–38. According to R. Voss, *Der Tanz und seine Geschichte. Eine kulturhistorisch-choreographische Studie.* Erfurt: Bartholomäus, 1868, p. 2, the Talmudist Christian August Vulpius claimed that the angels in paradise invented the dance, and humans took it from there.

9. Guttmann, *Ritual*, pp. 17, 19, 58.

10. C. Diem, *Weltgeschichte des Sports*, Stuttgart: Cotta, 1971 (3rd ed.), p. 3.

11. W. Eichel, "Die Entwicklung der Körperübungen in der Urgemeinschaft," in: *Theorie und Praxis der Körperkultur* 2 (1953), 1, 14–33.

12. F. Eppensteiner, *Der Sport, Wesen und Ursprung. Wert und Gestalt*, München: Reinhardt, 1964, pp. 50ff.

13. U. Popplow, "Aufgabe und Sinn einer Urgeschichte der Leibesübungen," in: *Leibeserziehung* 8 (1959), 10, 309–14;11, 353–58; 12, 382–90; *idem*, "Ursprung und Anfänge der Leibesübung," in: *Olympisches Feuer* 5 (1955), 1, 5–12; 2, 10–2 and 31.

14. Diem, *Weltgeschichte*, pp. 4–5.

15. Popplow, "Ursprung," 1, p. 10.

16. "This refers to a story of a Middle West farmer whose horse strayed out of its paddock. The farmer went into the middle of the paddock, chewed some grass, and asked himself: 'Now if I were a horse, where would I go?' " Quoted by M. Gluckman, *Politics, Law and Ritual in Tribal Society*. Oxford: Blackwell 1965, p. 2.

17. *Ibid.*

18. F. Engels. "Anteil der Arbeit an der Menschwerdung des Affen," *Marx-Engels-Werke*, vol. 20, Berlin: Dietz 1962, pp. 444.

19. G. Lukas, *Die Körperkultur in den frühen Epochen der Menschheitsentwicklung*. Berlin: Sportverlag, 1969, pp. 18ff.

20. *Idem.*, "Ursprung, Anfänge und frühe Formen der Körperübungen in der Urgesellschaft," in: W. Eichel (ed.), *Geschichte der Körperkultur in Deutschland*, vol. 1, Berlin: Sportverlag, 1969, p. 17.

21. R. D. Mandell, *Sport. A Cultural History*, New York: Columbia UP, 1984, p. 2.

22. J. Pasch (en), *Beschreibung wahrer Tanz-Kunst. Nebst einigen Anmerckungen über Herrn J.C.L.P.P. zu G. Bedenken gegen das Tantzen und zwar wo es als eine Kunst erkennet wird. Worinnen er zu behaupten vermeynet, dass das Tantzen/ wo es am besten ist/ nicht natürlich/ nicht vernünfftig/ nicht nützlich, sondern verdammlich/ und unzulässig sey*, Frankfurt: Michahelles & Adolph, 1707, p. 9.

23. F. M. Böhme, *Geschichte des Tanzes in Deutschland*. Leipzig: Breitkopf & Härtel, 1886, vol. 1. p. 1. The argument of Böhme is copied by J. Schikowski, *Geschichte des Tanzes*, Berlin: Büchergilde Gutenberg, 1926, p. 9.

24. M. von Boehn, *Der Tanz*, Berlin: Wegweiser, 1925, pp. 5ff.

25. E. Neuendorff. *Geschichte der neueren Deutschen Leibesübung*. Dresden: Limpert s.d. (1930), p. 1.

26. B. Saurbier and E. Stahr, *Geschichte der Leibesübungen*, Leipzig: Voigtländer 1939, p. 11.

27. Eppensteiner, *Der Sport*, p. 50.

28. A. Svahn, "Ursprung des Sports," in ICOSH (ed.), *Second International Seminar on History of Sport Science*, Magglingen: ETS, 1982, pp. 130–8.

29. A. Stevens, *Archetypes. A Natural History of the Self*, New York: Morrow, 1982, p. 24.

30. K. Wiemann, "Die Phylogenese menschlichen Verhaltens im Hinblick auf die Entwicklung sportlicher Betätigung," in H. Ueberhorst (ed.), *Geschichte*, vol. 1, pp. 48–63. It is surprising to note that both Guttmann, *Ritual*, p. 170 and Mandell, *Sport*, p. 308 have used Ueberhorst's previous chapter of the same book, but stopped reading at p. 47.

31. M. Meyer-Holzapfel, "Über die Bereitschaft zu Spiel und Instinkthandlungen," in *Zschft f. Tierpsych.* 13 (1956), 442–62; J. D. and J. I. Baldwin, "The Primate Contribution to the Study of Play," in: M. A. Salter (ed.), *Play. Anthropological Perspectives*, West Point, N.Y.: Leisure, 1978, pp. 53–68.

32. For reviews see: V. J. Harber and J. R. Sutton, "Endorphins and Exercise," in: *Sports Medicine* 1 (1984), 2, 154–71; J. Wildmann and A. Krüger, "Die Rolle endogener opioider Peptide beim Langstreckenlauf," in *Deutsche Zschft Sportmedizin* 37 (1986), 7, 201–10. For the role of rhythmical exercise, see J. L. Henry. "Circulating Opioids: Possible Physiological Roles in Central Nervous Function," in: *Neuroscience & Neurobehav. Rev.* 6 (1982), 229–45; A. Krüger and J. Wildmann. "Die Bedeutung der körpereigenen Opiate für den Leistungssport," in *Leistungssport* 15 (1985), 5, 49–54.

33. J. M. Griest et al., "Running as Treatment for Depression," in: *Comp. Psychi.*

20 (1979), 41–54; M. L. Sachs and G. W. Buffone, *Running as Therapy. An Integrated Approach*, Lincoln: Univ. of Nebraska Press, 1984.

34. J. Wildmann and A. Krüger et al., "Increase of Circulating Beta-Endorphine-like Immunoreactivity Correlates with the Change in the Feeling of Pleasantness," *Life Sciences* 38 (1986), 997–1003.

35. W. N. Taylor, *Anabolic Steroids and the Athlete*. Jefferson, N.C.: McFarlane, 1982, pp. 4ff.

36. B. Goldman, *Death in the Locker Room. Steroids & Sports*. South Bend, Ind.: Icarus, 1984; G. Hartmann, *Zur Wirkung von Testosteron und Training auf die Funktionsstrukturen des vegetativen Nervensystems*. Köln: Strauss 1985.

37. E. von Holst, *Zur Verhaltensphysiologie bei Tieren und Menschen*, München: Piper, 1969; A. Alland, *Evolution und menschliches Verhalten*, Frankfurt/M: S. Fischer, 1970; K. Lorenz: *Über tierisches und menschliches Verhalten*, München: Piper, 1965; V. Turner, "Body, Brain and Culture." in: *idem., On the Edge of the Bush. Anthropology of Experience*. Tuscon, Ariz.: Univ. of Arizona, 1985, pp. 349–73.

38. Id., "The New Neurosociology," in *ibid*. pp. 275–89. Cf. E. G. D'Aquili, *The Biopsychological Determinants of Culture*. Reading Mass.: Addison-Wesley, 1972; C. D. Laughlin and E. G. D'Aquili. *Biogenetic Structuralism*, New York: Columbia UP, 1974; E. O. Wilson, *Sociobiology: The New Synthesis*, Cambridge, Mass: Harvard UP, 1975; K. Lorenz, "The Psychobiological Approach: Methods and Results. Evolution of Ritualization in the Biological and Cultural Spheres," in Huxley, *Ritualization*, pp. 273–84.

39. Lukas, *Die Köperkultur*.

40. Weimann, "Phylogenese," p. 60.

41. Diem, *Weltgeschichte*.

42. Wiemann, "Phylogenese," p. 61.

43. J. Huxley (ed.), *A Discussion on Ritualization of Behaviour in Animals and Man. Philosophical Transactions of the Royal Society of London*. Ser. B. Biol. Sci. vol. 251, No. 772 (29 Dec. 1966), pp. 211–526.

44. V. Turner, "Body, Brain, and Culture," in: *idem, On the Edge of the Bush*, p. 272.

45. Huxley, "Introduction," in: *Ritualization*, p. 250.

46. R. B. Browne, *Rituals and Ceremonies in Popular Culture*. Bowling Green, Ohio: Bowling Green UP, 1980, p. 1.

47. C. D. Laughlin, J. McManus, and E. G. D'Aquili, "Introduction." in: D'Aquili, Laughlin, and McManus, *The Spectrum of Ritual. A Biogenetic Structural Analysis*. New York: Columbia UP, 1979, p. 5.

48. For example, E. Goffman. *Interaction Ritual*, Garden City, N.Y.: Doubleday, 1971. J. D. Saughnessy. *The Roots of Ritual*, Grand Rapids, Mich.: W. Eirdmans, 1973; E. R. Leach, "Ritual," in: *International Encyclopedia of the Social Sciences*, New York: Macmillan and Freepress, 1968, vol. 13, pp. 520–6; E. A. Fischer, "Le rituel comme moyen de communication," in: *Questions Liturgiques* 52 (1971), 3, pp. 197–215.

49. E. R. Leach, "Ritualization in Man. Ritualization in Man in Relation to Conceptual and Social Development," in: Huxley, *Ritualization*, p. 403.

50. As the latest example, cf. R. Dawkins. *The Blind Watchmaker. Why the Evidence of Evolution Reveals a Universe Without Design*, London: Norton 1986.

51. Laughlin, McManus, and D'Aquili, "Introduction," p. 5.

52. *Ibid.*, p. 29.

53. O. E. Klapp, *Ritual and Cult*, Annals of American Sociology, Washington, D.C.: Public Affairs Pr., 1956.

54. A. O. Dunleavy and A. W. Miracle. "Sport: An Experimental Setting for the Development of a Theory of Ritual," in: A. T. Cheska (ed.), *Play as Context*, West Point, N.Y.: Leisure, 1981, pp. 118–26. They analyze particularly the cohesive and coordinative, the communication, the changes in state, and the adjustive response to stress functions.

55. S. Kilmer, "Sport as Ritual. A Theoretical Approach," in: D. F. Lancy and B. A. Tindall (eds.), *The Study of Play: Problems and Prospects*. West Point, N.Y.: Leisure, 1977, pp. 44–9.

56. F. Staal, "The Meaninglessness of Ritual," in: *Numen 26* (1979), pp. 2–22. For a structuralist critique that does not feel that a new paradigm is necessary, cf. H. H. Penner, "Language, Ritual and Meaning," in: *Numen 32* (1982), pp. 1–16.

57. Cf. J. Bentley, *Ritualism and Politics* in *Victorian Britian. The Attempt to Legislate Belief*. Oxford: OUP, 1978.

58. Cf. P. de Coubertin, *Pedagogie sportive*, Paris: Vrin, 1972, pp. 152ff.; idem, *Der olympische Gedanke. Reden und Aufsätze*, Schorndorf: Hofmann, 1967, p. 67 (Lettres olympiques 4, Dec. 1918, No. VI); idem, "La valeur pédagogique du cérémonial olympique," in: *Bull. Bureau Int. Péd. Sport*. No. 7 s.d. (1932), pp. 3–5; idem, "Décoration, Pyrotechnic, Harmonies, Cortèges," in: *Rév. Olympique*, April 1911, pp. 54–9; May 1911, pp. 71–6; July 1911, pp. 106–10; August 1911, pp. 122–5; October 1911, pp. 149–53. A. Krüger, "Neo-Olympismus zwischen Nationalismus und Internationalismus," in: Ueberhorst, *Geschichte*, vol. 3/1, 1980, pp. 522–68; J. J. MacAloon, *This Great Symbol*, Chicago: Univ. of Chicago Press, 1981; H. Lenk, *Werte, Ziele, Wirklichkeit der modernen Olympischen Spiele,* Schorndorf: Hofmann, 1964; Q. Wright, "Symbols of Nationalism and Internationalism," in: *Symbols and Values. An Initial Study*. 13th Symposium of the Conference on Science, Philosophy and Religion, New York, 1954, pp. 383–403.

59. Cf. A. Krüger, *Die Olympischen Spiele 1936 und die Weltmeinung*, Berlin: Bartels & Wernitz, 1972; R. D. Mandell, *The Nazi Olympics*, New York: Columbia UP, 1971; H. Bernett, "Symbolik und Zeremoniell der XI. Olympischen Spiele in Berlin 1936," in: *Sportwissenschaft* 16 (1986), 4, pp. 357–97; H. Eichberg, M. Dultz, et al., *Massenspiele—NS Thingspiele, Arbeiterweihespiel und olympisches Zeremoniell*, Stuttgart-Bad Cannstadt: Frommann-Holzbog, 1977; T. Alkemeyer, "Gewalt und Opfer im Ritual der Olympischen Spiele 1936," in: W. Dressen (ed.), *Selbstbeherrschte Körper*, Berlin: Museumspädagogischer Dienst, 1986, pp. 60–77.

60. MacAloon, *Great Symbol*, p. 270. He refers to the theory developed by A. van Gennep, *Rites de Passage*, Chicago: Chicago UP, 1960, furthered by V. Turner, *The Forest of Symbols*, Ithaca, N.Y.: Cornell UP, 1967 and idem, *The Ritual Process. Structure and Anti-Structure*, Chicago: Aldine, 1969; cf. N. Sindzingre, "Rites de passage," in: *Encyclopaedia Universalis,* Paris: Larousse, 1985, pp. 1158–60. The same theory was applied to American football earlier to a far greater extent by M. J. Deegan; M. Stein, "American Drama and Ritual: Nebraska Football," in: *IRSS* 13 (1978), 3, pp. 31–44.

61. E. D. Chapple and C. S. Coon, *Principles of Anthopology*, New York: H. Holt, 1942.

62. J.-M. Bröhm, *Le mythe olympique*, Paris: Ch. Bourgois, 1981, pp. 55ff.

63. *Idem*, "Le corps: un paradigme de la modernité," in: *Actions et Recherches*

Sociales 18 (March 1985), 1, 15–38; M. Mauss, *Sociologie et anthropologie,* Paris: PUF, 1950; therein see also the introduction by C. Lévi-Strauss; M. Foucault, "Pouvoir et corps," in J.-M. Bröhm (ed.), *Quel corps?* Paris: Ed. de la Passion, 1986, pp. 61–8; M. Bernard, *Le corps,* Paris: Ed. Univ., 1972. For the French positions, cf. J. Cazeneuve, "Rites," pp. 1156–8 and N. Sindzingre, "Rituels," pp. 1160–3, in: *Encyclopaedia Universalis,* Paris: Larousse 1985.

64. Laughlin et al., *Introduction,* pp. 40f.

65. E. D. Chapple, *Culture and Biological Man.* New York: Holt, Rinehart & Winston, 1970.

66. J. McManus, "Ritual and Ontogenetic Development," in: D'Aquili et al., *Spectrum,* p. 206; H. M. Schroder, M. Driver, and S. Streufert, *Human Information Processing.* New York: Holt, Rinehart & Winston, 1967.

67. A.Taylor Cheska, "Sports Spectacular: A Ritual Model of Power," in: *Int. Rev. Sp. Soc.* 14 (1979), 2, 51–72; for a nonsporting context, cf. R. L. Grimes, "Organizing and Symbolizing Power," in: *idem, Symbols and Conquest,* Ithaca, N.Y.: Cornell UP, 1976, pp. 91–151.

68. R. Lipsyte, *Sportsworld. An American Dreamland,* New York: New York Times Books, 1975; D. Q. Voigt, "American Sporting Ritual," in: Browne, *Rituals and Ceremonies,* pp. 127–9; K. Egger, *Lernübertragungen in der Sportpädagogik. Bildungstheoretische, methodologische und lernpsychologische Aspekte des Transferproblems im Sportunterricht,* Basel: Birkhäuaser 1975.

69. B. W. Lex, "The Neurobiology of Ritual Trance," in: D'Aquili et al., *Spectrum,* pp. 117–51; for a sociophilosophical interpretation, cf. T. Luckmann, "Riten als Bewältigung lebensweltlicher Grenzen," in: *Schweiz. Z. Soziol.* 3 (1985), pp. 535–50.

70. Henry, "Circulating Opioids," *op. cit.*

71. H. Akil, S. J. Watson, et al., "Endogenous Opioids: Biology and Function," in: *Ann. Rev. Neurosci.* 7 (1984), pp. 223–55; A. I. Basbaum and H. L. Fields, "Endogenous Pain Control Systems: Brainstem Spinal Pathways and Endorphin Circuitry," in: *Ann. Rev. Neurosci.* 7 (1984), pp. 309–38.

72. C. Gorlier, "Rituali dell'età technologia," in: *Paragone* (Firence) 20 (1969), No. 228, pp. 13–36.

73. J. C. Willer, H. Dehen, and J. Cambier, "Stress-induced Analgesia in Humans: Endogenous Opioids and Naloxone-Reversible Depression of Pain Reflexes," in: *Science* 212 (1981), pp. 689–91; A. Pfeiffer and A. Herz, "Endocrine Actions of Opioids," in: *Horm. metabol. Res.* 16 (1984), pp. 386–97; R. T. Ross and A. Randich, "Unconditioned Stress-Induced Analgesia Following Exposure to Brief Footshocks," in *J. Exp. Psych.* 10 (1984), 2, pp. 127–37; S. Amir, Z. Brown, and Z. Amit, "The Role of Endorphins in Stress: Evidence and Speculations," *Neurosci & Biobeh Rev.* 4 (1980), pp. 77–86.

74. A. Krüger and J. Wildmann, in *Leistungssport, op.cit.*

75. C. D. Laughlin and E. G. D'Aquili, "Ritual and Stress," in: D'Aquili et al., *Spectrum,* p. 280.

76. E. Shils, "Ritual and Crisis," in Huxley, *Ritualization,* pp. 447–50.

77. Guttmann, *Ritual,* pp. 16ff. uses S. Culin, *Games of the North American Indians,* Washington, D.C.: U.S. Govt. Printing Office 1907, only to show how religion actually played a role in Indian games. He did not look for quantifications, or he would have found among other things the following: "In winter . . . the children of both sexes gather in the kashim, and each child in succession spins its top. The moment the top is spun the owner runs out through the entrence passage and attempts to make a complete circuit

of the house and enter again before the top stops spinning. A score is made every time this is done successfully,'' pp. 738f. (quoted from *The Eskimo about Bering Strait,* 1899, p. 333).

78. A. Guttmann, *Sports Spectators,* New York: Columbia UP, 1986; cf. E. L. Rosseau, "Great American Ritual: Watching games'' in: *Nation* 187 (1958), 4, pp. 188–91: the paradox of the interaction between spectators and participants, the ritual and actual practice, is described by M. Bernard, "Le spectacle sportif. Les paradoxes du spectacle sportif ou les ambiguïtés de la compétition théâtralisée,'' in: C. Pociello (ed.), *Sport et société. Approche socioculturelle des pratiques,* Paris: Vigot, 1981, pp. 353–60; the argument of E. Dunning, P. Murphy, and J. Williams, "Spectator violence at football matches: Towards a sociological explanation,'' in: N. Elias and E. Dunning, *Quest for Excitement. Sport and Leisure in the Civilizing Process,* Oxford: B. Blackwell, 1986, pp. 245–66, particularly pp. 252f. on ritualized aggression points to the conclusion that former pan-species instincts and rituals are still active and understood on the level of the subculture.

79. One should, however, not overlook the fact that often the ritual is staged for the benefit of the spectator as in free style wrestling. Cf. for other settings D. MacCannell, "Staged Authenticity: Arrangements of Social Space in Tourist Settings,'' in: *AJS* 79 (1974), 3, pp. 589–603; A. Goldberg, "Play and Ritual in Haitian Voodoo Shows for Tourists,'' in: J. Loy (ed.), *The Paradoxes of Play,* West Point, N.Y.: Leisure, 1982, pp. 42–9.

80. *For individual ritual,* see G. J. Gmelch, "Baseball magic,'' in: *Trans-Actions* 8 (1971), pp. 39–41, 54: C. J. Gregory and B. M. Petrie, "Superstitions of Canadian Intercollegiate Athletes. An Inter-sport Comparison,'' in: *IRSS* 10 (1975), 2, pp. 59–68; J. Becker, "Superstition in sport,'' *Int. J. Sport Psych* 6 (1975), pp. 148–52.

For team ritual, see K. Larson, " 'Keep Up the Chatter': Ritual Communications in American Summer Softball,'' Paper presented at the annual meeting of the Am. Anthrop. Assoc., Washington, D.C.; M. Stein, "Cult and Sport. The Case of Big Red,'' in: *Mid-West Rev of Soc* 2 (1977), 2, pp. 29–42; W. Arens, "The Great American Football Ritual,'' in: *Natural History* 84 (1975), pp. 72–80; J. A. Beran, "The Iowa Girls' High School Basketball Tournament Viewed as an Institutionalized Ritual,'' in: Cheska, *Play as Context,* pp. 149–57: M. J. Deegan; G. G. Watson and T. M. Kando, "The Meaning of Rules and Rituals in Little League Baseball,'' in: *Pacif Soc Rev.* 19 (1976), 3, 291–315; O. Patterson, "The Cricket Ritual in the West Indies,'' in: *New Society* 352 (June 1969), pp. 988–9.

For interpretations, see G. A. Fine, "Small Groups and Sport: A Symbolic Interactionist Perspective,'' in: C. R. Rees and A. W. Miracle (eds.), *Sport and Social Theory,* Champaign, Ill.: Human Kinetics, 1986, pp. 159–70; J. C. Harris, "Sport and Ritual: A Macroscopic Comparison of Form,'' in: J. Loy, *The Paradoxes of Play,* West Point, N.Y.: Leisure, 1982, pp. 205–14, revised in idem, and R. J. Park (eds.), *Play, Games & Sports in Cultural Contexts,* Champaign, Ill., *Human Kinetics* 1983, pp. 177–89; A. T. Cheska, "Sports Spectacular: The Social Ritual of Power,'' in *Quest* (1978), no. 30, pp. 58–71; J. H. Duthie, "Athletics: The Ritual of a Technological Society?'', in: H. B. Schwartzmann (ed.), *Play and Culture,* West Point, N.Y.: Leisure, 1980, pp. 91–8; A. Miracle, "Functions of School Athletics: Boundary Maintenance and System Integration,'' in: M. Salter (ed.), *Play,* pp. 176–86; M. Novak, "Game's the Thing. In Defence of Sports as Ritual,'' in: *Columbia Journalism Rev* (May 15, 1976), pp. 33–8.

81. The same opinion is H. Lenk, ''Tra rito, etica e mito,'' in: *Lancilotto e Nausica* 4 (1987), 1, pp. 20–31.

82. Turner, ''The New Neurosociology,'' in: *idem, On the Edge of the Bush,* pp. 275–89.

83. Laughlin and D'Aquili, ''Ritual and Stress,'' p. 307.

Rituals, Records, Responses

ALLEN GUTTMANN

The day after he published *Don Juan,* commented Lord Byron, he awoke to find himself famous. Wise scholars about to publish the results of their research reconcile themselves to a less spectacular reception than that accorded Byron's comic poem. When a work of scholarship reaches beyond the narrow circle of specialists, which seems to have been the case with *From Ritual to Record,* the author should be grateful for negative as well as for positive criticism. The only proviso is that the criticism be perceptive and not simply the irritable result of a failure to take the work seriously. Since most of the chapters contained in the present collection offer an essentially negative—but nonetheless serious—critique of the Eichberg-Mandell-Guttmann view of the uniqueness of modern sports, I welcome the opportunity to respond.

The first thing that needs to be said is that Carter and Krüger are correct to observe, as they do in the introduction to this book, that Eichberg, Mandell, and I have many scholarly disagreements. This should surprise nobody. What we agree on is that modern sports are a unique, socially constructed phenomenon whose most distinctive features are an extraordinary degree of quantification and an obsession with the sports record. Whether modern sports were born in Italy and France at the time of the Renaissance, in Restoration England, in seventeenth-century Japan, or in the academies of the German *Philanthropen* at the end of the eighteenth century is, in my view, a secondary question (and one quite unlikely to be settled definitively). The most important question, at least as it relates to my work and to Mandell's, concerns the formal-structural characteristics of modern sports compared to those of previous ages. What, in the overly simplified terms that I used in the title of this chapter and that seem to have taken on a life of their own, is the relationship between ritual and record?

Before I can deal with that question, I must comment on the methodological attack mounted by Parkerson. His charge that I ignore "sport as a developmental process" misses the point because I never attempted to trace the development of sports from antiquity to modern times.[1] I sought rather to emphasize the extraordinary differences between modern sports and those of earlier times, and my approach was consciously more taxonomic than diachronic, which is why I organized my argument thematically rather than by historical periods. Parkerson's little two-by-two table for verification or falsification of theories, of which he seems excessively proud, makes the obvious point that a theory is not useful unless it can somehow be falsified by contradictory evidence. I agree. Since most of the chapters in the present collection insist that the evidence *has* falsified the Eichberg-Mandell-Guttmann theory about the uniqueness of modern sports, it cannot logically be the case that *both* Parkerson *and* our other critics are right. In fact, he is wrong and the other contributors to this volume of criticism are partly right.

Parkerson's own attempt to prove my views false on the basis of the empirical evidence represents a serious failure to understand the Weberian ideal type as a heuristic paradigm. Among his hectoring rhetorical questions are these:

How many polo players are poor? What is the socioeconomic status of professional golfers? Certainly no poor folks here. These are just a few examples of rampant age, gender, class, and race equalities within sport today which are apparently unimportant in Guttmann's scheme of things.

What I wrote under the rubric of equality was this: "In actual practice, there are numerous inequalities, which will occupy us at some length when we consider not the conceptual model but the contemporary state of affairs."[2] I did discuss a number of these inequalities in *From Ritual to Record* and in my subsequent books and essays. What Parkerson fails to comprehend is that the ideal-type method, as explained and exemplified in Max Weber's *Wirtschaft und Gesellschaft,* is a heuristic device that enables a scholar to assess the inevitable difference between the ideal and the actual. Although he seems unaware of the fact, Parkerson's own description of the ideal social scientist is a Weberian construct of this type. Where does Parkerson propose—except in the realm of the ideal—to find the paragon who will satisfy the criterion that he present "all the evidence" for an interpretation of sports history that ranges from preliterate cultures to modern times? Parkerson's strictures can no more be taken as a guide to real-world research than the remarks in the Carter-Krüger introduction to the effect that medievalists should know Greek, Latin, Hebrew, English, French, German, Italian, Polish, Provençal, Russian, Swedish, and Arabic. In short, Parkerson's sarcastic remarks prove only that he is probably not the appropriate person to give lessons in scientific historiography.

The empirically based criticisms of my work are more substantial. My argument, originally set forth in *From Ritual to Record: The Nature of Modern Sports* (1978), is that the characteristics of modern sports—secularism, equality, specialization, rationalization, bureaucratization, quantification, and the quest for records—"interact systematically."[3] Since some critics mistakenly assumed that I had asserted that the presence or absence of the concept of the sports record was in itself sufficient to characterize a sport as modern or not, I repeated my point in *A Whole New Ball Game* (1988): "In considering this proposed set of characteristics, one must bear in mind that they are not a random collection. They interact systematically."[4]

I see in retrospect, however, that I brought a good deal of trouble on myself by choosing an allusive and apparently elusive title. The phrase "from ritual to record" is actually an allusion to Jessie Weston's famous study of the primitive rituals that allegedly lay behind the medieval romance.[5] No one has ever, to the best of my knowledge, assumed that Weston meant to deny the persistence of ritual in the romance. "If you follow the title of Allen Guttmann's famous book," writes Arnd Krüger in his chapter on ritual in modern sport, it "is doubtful whether there are any rituals left." True. But I expected responsible readers to continue beyond the title, and Krüger, who has apparently read the complete book, acknowledges my awareness of the existence of modern rituals, including sports rituals. Indeed, a number of them are referred to in *From Ritual to Record*.[6] The important difference, made plain in the text of my work, is that modern sports rituals are secular and not sacred. Since the main point of my next book, *The Games Must Go On* (1984), was that Avery Brundage conceived of the Olympic Games as a secular religion, it is bothersome that some critics still believe that I doubt the existence of the ritual aspects of modern sports. In fact, I agree completely with Krüger's assertion that ritual and record exist "side by side" in modern sports.

If the confusion brought on by a fixation on my title rather than on my text has now been removed, we are free to evaluate the truly serious criticisms made by Decker, Ramba, Carter, Rühl, McClelland, Ito, and Gundolf Krüger, all of whom allege that quantification, the mania for records, or both existed prior to the modern era.

Decker, the acknowledged expert in the field of Egyptian sports history, has proven to my satisfaction that an attempt was made to quantify the sports achievements of the Eighteenth-Dynasty pharaohs and that Egyptian sources attest to a quantifiable progression from the ritual archery performances of Thutmosis III to those of Amenophis II. Whether such a progression deserves the name of a sports record remains debatable. Four or five instances of quantified achievement (without the possibility of standardization) are suggestive rather than conclusive. More importantly, the royal dogma required the pharaoh to be the physical representative of the power and glory of Egypt. It was, therefore, unthinkable that the pharaoh compete in a sports contest that he might lose. The only possible competition is a preordained one between the pharaoh and his predecessor, who is always vanquished, or between the pharaoh and his earlier self, who is always surpassed. The inevitable question arises: were these true contests or were they simply a form of propaganda? In fact, modern efforts to replicate the fabulous deeds of Amenophis II have resulted in miserable failure; not only did the arrows *not* transfix the copper sheets, but they penetrated only a few millimeters.[7] As Decker rightly comments, we must be quite skeptical about the historicity of these fabled achievements. The mature pharaoh's feats of archery may have been as much the product of a fabulous imagination as the young prince's 37-meter high jump.[8] We are left with the fact that it was important to the Egyptians to believe that the pharaoh's achievements were unprecedented. Whether this fact alone justifies the claim that Egyptian ritual included the modern sports record is, in my view, problematical, but there was admittedly a closer approach than I realized before the publication of Decker's important book.

Ramba's discussion of "recordmania" in Greek and Roman sports is much less persuasive for two reasons. He is surprisingly gullible about the Greek evidence, and he is disappointingly careless in his misrepresentation of my account of both the Greek and the Roman texts. Ramba asserts that the Greeks were given to quantified boasts about the number of times they had won this or that event. Indeed, they were, and I acknowledged as much when I wrote, "The closest approach to our modern sense of quantification was in the numeration of achievements. Just as Herakles performed ten labors, Milo of Croton was famed for five victories at Olympia, six at the Pythian games, ten at the Isthmian games, and nine at Nemea."[9]

Ramba also makes much of quantified distances and weights, but his examples of quantification are highly questionable. He cites the fabled feat of Phayllus the Croton, which I discussed in *From Ritual to Record*.[10] The epigram says that Phayllus jumped 55 feet and threw the discus 95 feet. It is, however, doubtful that the epigram referred to an actual event. At any rate, a jump of 55 feet is nearly twice the distance of Bob Beamon's still unmatched 1968 record. Hermodius of Lampsakos is another questionable case. That he actually lifted a rock weighing 480 kilograms is very unlikely. Neither these nor the other well-known numbers cited by Ramba can be taken literally. Like the fabulous numbers given by Herodotus in his *History of the Persian Wars* (e.g., that King Xerxes led an invading army of 1.7 million men), such claims actually demonstrate how little the Greeks were concerned about accurate numbers.

If we credit these highly questionable reports, we are nonetheless confronted with fact that the Greek concept of equality in sports was very limited. They did apparently have starting blocks and a mechanism to prevent runners from"jumping the gun," but they had no way to record precise times and thus no way to make comparisons (and thus no way to set records in races). Comparability between races run at different festivals was doomed because the stadia were of different lengths. A "stade race" was for 177.5 meters at Delphi, and for 210 meters at Pergamon. Although the contestants in the discus and javelin events presumably used the same equipment, the Greeks lacked standardized measures for distance. Since the "foot" varied from place to place, comparison was, once again, impossible except *an Ort und Stelle*. If Ramba implies some kind of standardization of the discus, he is clearly wrong. As I indicated in my original discussion, "the diameters of discuses which have come down to us vary from 5.5 inches to 13.5 inches and the weights from 3 to 15 pounds."[11] Given the extremely limited possibilities for quantified comparisons of any sort (other than the number of victories), M. I. Finley and W. H. Pleket concluded that there was no way for the Greeks to express the concepts "to set a record" or "to break the record."[12] There is no good reason to challenge their conclusion.

Unlike the scattered and unreliable evidence of quantification in Greek sports, documentation for Roman sports is impressively large. My response to the detailed data gathered by Ramba is simple. He seeks to disprove an assertion I never made. Neither I nor any other sports historian has claimed, to the best of my knowledge, that the Romans did not quantify the results of their chariot races or count the number of victories in gladiatorial combat. What I actually said was this:

... the Romans became fascinated with counting the number of first places, second places, first places won from behind, etc. There is, for instance, an inscription to Gaius Apuleius Diocles, whose career began in 122 A.D. In four-horse chariot races, he started 4,527 times, won 1,462 times, came in second 861 times, and third 576 times. . . . There was a second kind of quantification which began under the Greeks and continued into Roman times. Professional athletes frequently boasted that they were the first to have won seven victories at seven different festivals or three times in a row at this or that famous site. It is still a long way from this type of scoring to the lengthy statistical appendices with which modern biographies terminate, but the first steps were taken.[13]

This characteristic—quantification of results—was "seized upon and developed *almost* in the spirit of modern sports."[14] If Ramba is correct that our mutual friend Gaius Apuleius Diocles was acclaimed because he exceeded the quantified performances of his rivals, then I must acknowledge error and admit that, in chariot races if not in other sports, the Romans anticipated the modern sports record. Whether we can then go on to say that their approach to sports in general was systematically comparable to ours is an open question.

The medieval case can be dealt with more briefly. Carter has assembled an impressive array of evidence about the sports and pastimes of the Middle Ages, but very little of his evidence refers specifically to the sports record because recording data are not at all the same as setting and breaking records. As I have attempted repeatedly to explain, the modern sports record is an unsurpassed but presumably surpassable quantified achievement.[15] This use of the term *record*, derived from the phrase "the best recorded achievement," first appears in English in the midnineteenth century. It is first attested by an English dictionary in 1883. When the poetic biography of William Marshal tells us that Marshal's contemporaries said of his exploits that "never was such a feat seen or heard of from a single knight," we have the kind of superlative speech that occurs in many cultures and in many historical periods. Such speech says nothing about a sports record. *If,* however, Carter is correct about a medieval reference to 500 knights captured, *if,* furthermore, subsequent knights emulated the redoubtable Marshal and attempted to surpass him by the capture of more than 500 knights, *then*— and only then—will we have an instance of the modern concept of a sports record. To assert on the basis of this solitary datum from a work of poetic narrative that the Middle Ages were in any respect modern in their approach to sports is a step I am not yet ready to make.

Rühl's account of the point system of the medieval tournament is quite another. He is right. I was wrong. Here is obviously a case of sports quantification which had been overlooked by historians at the time I wrote my book. For that matter, this side of the joust is *still* overlooked by the specialists in medieval studies.[16] Having the benefit of Rühl's researches, one can now ask more precise questions about the *degree* of quantification. Although it seems that both the *tenants* and the *venants* charged the same number of times, fifty-seven in Rühl's example, there seems to have been no effort within a side to equalize the number of charges. The duke of Buckingham charged seventeen times, and Lord Berners only eight. For the duke then to receive the prize, as he did, seems on the face of it to violate our modern sense of equal treatment within the rules of the game. Whether or not any attempt was made to compare scores from one tournament to another, and thus to approach the concept of the sports record, is unclear from Rühl's treatment.

We come then to the Renaissance, a period which Eichberg and Mandell have discussed but which I had neglected prior to the publication of *Sports Spectators* (1986). If one emphasizes the rationalization and quantification of *calcio* and places less stress on the geometric-aesthetic aspects of Renaissance sports, then a case can be made for Italy and France as the birthplace of modern sports, but McClelland is much more cautious now than he was in his contributions to *Die Anfänge des modernen Sports in der Renaissance* (1984), which he edited together with Arnd Krüger.[17] He no longer maintains that geometry is an example of quantification (although, of course, it *is* an example of the "mathematization" of sports). He no longer claims, as he seemed to in the earlier collection, that the example of antiquity inspired Renaissance men to "a hunt for records."[18] His discussion of the precise degree of quantification possible in a culture that had not yet standardized its weights and measures is excellent. His conclusion that "Renaissance sports stand astride a nexus of competing and often contradictory intellectual and social trends" is one with which I heartily agree. Although I continue to believe that the development of the formal-structural characteristics of modern sports can best be traced to England in the late seventeenth century, I now understand that a strong case can be made for the Renaissance. A great deal depends, of course, on *how* one defines modern sports, that is, on *which* formal-structural characteristics one selects as definitive.

Although I have spent a good deal of the last decade in a less than wholly successful effort to learn Japanese, I am reluctant to respond directly to the contribution by Ito and Krüger. Their critique concentrates on the work of Eichberg and Mandell, and Eichberg has replied to their criticisms. (His point was essentially that isolated instances can always be located but that they do not always interact systematically.)[19] The original publication of the Ito-Krüger essay encouraged me to return to some speculations on Japanese archery which appeared in *From Ritual to Record*.[20] In a 1983 essay, I raised the possibility that at least *some* of the characteristics of modern sports emerged in Japan, quite independently of European influence, as early as the seventeenth century.

Although the modern archery target does not seem to have been invented independently by Islamic or Hindu or Confucian culture, the Japanese may have anticipated the Dutch and the French. Seventeenth-century illustrations of the Japanese classic, *The Tale of Genji*, show the courtiers of Kyoto shooting at what are unmistakably modern targets. In fact, documentary evidence suggests that the archery contest at Kyoto's Sanjusangen-do Temple may have been—as early as the seventeenth century—attempts to set quantified records. In other words, while Persian and Turkish archers were still content to fire away at the gabaq or gourd mounted upon a mast, the Japanese seem to have invented the modern sport of archery. What this possibility suggests to me is that the stunningly rapid modernization of Japan in the late nineteenth century was the result of factors long present in Japanese culture. Even if it were shown that the modern target was introduced to Japan by the Dutch, who were allowed to carry on a minimal trade with Japan even after the islands had shut themselves off from the West, it is still important to recognize that the Japanese were receptive to this abstraction while Persians and Turks preferred less abstract and more representational gourds, melons, bags, and baskets.[21]

This admittedly speculative line of analysis fits nicely with the *chikaraisha* data cited by Ito and Krüger. I am intrigued enough to want to pursue the matter further, but the dominance of *sumo*, a sport suffused with Shinto ritual, will inevitably qualify whatever claims I or anyone else will wish to make about modernization and Japanese sports.

I am not competent to offer a judgment on the sociobiological argument set forth in the last chapter of the present collection, but this hardly matters because Arnd Krüger is only tangentially concerned here with the Eichberg-Mandell-Guttmann thesis. Krüger may, however, be interested to know that an American classicist, David Sansone, has recently published a book of a somewhat similar tendency, *Greek Athletics and the Genesis of Sport* (1988). Building on Walter Burkert's *Homo Necans* (1972) and drawing also on sociobiologists like Konrad Lorenz, Sansone—like Krüger—understands sports as ritualized behavior in the service of human biological needs.

In the course of his sociobiological argument, Krüger gives a curious turn to the historical debate about the origins of modern sports. If sports are a ritual means to cope with "ecological stress," which I take to be Krüger's main point, then it is quite reasonable for him to conclude, as he seems to, that "modern sports arose in Britain" because Britain was "the first industrial society," but this new position certainly represents a considerable modification of his earlier views on the Renaissance origins of modern sports. As I have already noted, McClelland, too, has modified *his* position. Having acknowledged my own readiness to revise some of my untenable remarks, for example, my claims about the lack of quantification in medieval sports, I perceive a kind of convergence of views—at least among some of the participants in the debate. Scholarship is not and should not be a zero-sum game.

NOTES

1. This task was attempted by Richard Mandell in *Sport: A Cultural History* (New York: Columbia University Press, 1984).

2. *From Ritual to Record* (New York: Columbia University Press, 1978), p. 26.

3. Ibid., p. 54.

4. *A Whole New Ball Game* (Chapel Hill: University of North Carolina Press, 1988), p. 7.

5. Jessie Weston, *From Ritual to Romance* (Cambridge: Cambridge University Press, 1920).

6. *From Ritual to Record*, pp. 41–42.

7. The facts are much clearer in Decker's original discussion; see Wolfgang Decker, *Sport und Spiel im alten Aegypten* (Munich: C. W. Beck, 1987), p. 54.

8. Ibid., p. 117.

9. *From Ritual to Record*, p. 50.

10. Ibid., p. 49.

11. Ibid., p. 43.

12. M. I. Finley and W. H. Pleket, *The Olympic Games* (New York: Viking Press, 1976), p. 22.

13. *From Ritual to Record*, p. 50.

14. Ibid.

15. For the exchange of views, see *The Journal of Sport History* 6:7 (Summer 1979): 87–92.

16. See Juliet V. Barker, *The Tournament in England, 1100–1400* (Woodbridge, Suffolk: Boydell Press, 1986).

17. For my review, see *Sportwissenschaft* 17:1 (1987): 98–99.

18. John McClelland, *Die Anfänge des modernen Sports in der Renaissance* (London: Arena, 1984), p. 11.

19. See Henning Eichberg, "Recording and Quantifying Performance Is Not Natural: A Reply to Krüger and Ito," *Stadion* 3:2 (1977): 253–56. The 1977 volume appeared in 1979.

20. *From Ritual to Record*, pp. 53–54.

21. "Sociology, Sport, and Popular Literature," *Sport and the Sociological Imagination*, Nancy Theberge and Peter Donnelly, eds. (Fort Worth: Texas Christian University Press, 1983), p. 11.

Selected Bibliography

BIBLIOGRAPHIES

CONI. Biblioteca sportiva nazionale (Ed.). *Catalogo delle opere dei secoli XVI–XVII–XVII*. Roma: CONI, 1981.

Decker, Wolfgang. *Annotierte Bibliographie zum Sport im Alten Ägypten*. St. Augustin: Richarz, 1978 with followups in *Stadion* 5,2 (1979), 161–192; 7, 2 (1981), 153–172; 8/9(1982/3), 193–214: *Nikephoros* 1(1988), 245–268.

Krüger, Arnd, and John McClelland. "Ausgewählte Bibliographie zu Leibesübungen und Sport in der Renaissance." In idem (ed.), *Die Anfänge des Modernen Sports in der Renaissance*. London: Arena, 1984, 132–180.

Lovesey, Peter, and Tom McNab. *The Guide to British Track and Field Literature. 1275–1968*. London: Arena, 1969.

Moroda, Derra de. *The Dance Library. 1480–1980. A Catalogue*. München: R. Wölfle, 1982.

Sweet, W. E. *Sport and Recreation in Ancient Greece: A Sourcebook*. Oxford: Oxford UP, 1987.

Tannenbaum, Samuel A., and Dorothy R. *Elizabethan Bibliographies*. Port Washington, N.Y.: Kennikat, 1967ff.

Thimm, Carl A. *Bibliography of Fencing and Duelling*. Bronx, N.Y.: Benjamin Blom, 1896. (Reissued 1968.)

Wright, Lyle H. *Sporting Books in the Huntington Library*. San Marino, Calif.: Huntington, 1937.

SOURCES AND SOURCE COLLECTIONS

Ascham, Roger. *Toxophilus. The schole of shootinge conteyned in two bookes*. London: Whytchurch, 1545. (Reprint New York: Da Capo, 1969.)

er.

l

. Milano: Il

llee

Bardi, Giovanni. *Discorso sopra il giuoco del calcio fiorentino*. Firenze: Giunti, 1580.
Bascetta, Carlo. *Sport e Giuochi: Trattati et scritti dal XV al XVIII secolo*. Milano: Il Polifilo, 1978.
Bender, Johann Georg. *Kurzer Unterricht dess lobwürdigen Exercitii dess Ballen-Spiels*. Nürnberg: A. Knorzen, 1680.
Culin, Stewart. *Games of the North American Indians. 24th Annual Report of the Bureau of American Ethnology to the Smithsonian Institute. 1902–1903*. Washington, D.C.: Government Printing Office, 1907. (Reprint New York: Dover, 1975.)
Dilich, Wilhelm. *Historische Beschreibung der Fürstlichen Kindtauff Fräwlin Elisabethen zu Hessen*. Kassel: Wessel, 1598. (Reprint as *Ritterspiele–Anno 1596*. Kassel: George Wenderoth, 1986.)
Hulpeau, Charles. *Le jeu royal de la paume*. Paris: C. Hulpeau, 1632.
Markham, Gervase. *The Art of Archerie*. London: B. Fisher, 1634.
Menestrier, Claude Fracois. *Traité des tournois, iovstes, carrousels et autres spectacles publics*. Lyon: M. Mayer, 1674.
Neade, William. *The double-arms man by the new invention. Briefly shewing some famous exploits atchievedd by our British bowmen*. London: Grismand, 1625. (Reprint Menston: Scolar, 1971.)
N. N. *Chronik alter Kampfkünste. Zeichnungen und Texte aus Schriften alter Meister entstanden 1443–1674*. Berlin: Weinmann, 1986.
Scaino, Antonio. *Trattato del giuoco della palla*. Venezia: Ferrari, 1555.
Tucarro, Arcangelo. *Trois Dialogues de L'exercice de sauter et voltiger en l'air*. Paris: Claude de Monstr'oeil, 1599. (Reprint Alburgh: Archival Facsimiles, 1987.)
Vulson de la Colombière, Marc. *Le vrai theatre d'honneur et de chevalerie ou le mirroir heroique de la noblesse, contenant les combats ou jeux sacrez . . . les tournois, les joustes, . . . les combats à la barriere, les carrousels, les courses de bague et de la quintaine*. Paris: A. Courbé, 1648.

SECONDARY LITERATURE

D'Allemagne, Henri-René. *Sport et jeux d'adresse*. Paris: Hachette, 1903.
Anglo, Sidney. "Archives of the English Tournament: Score Checks and Lists." *J. Soc. Archivists* 2(1961), 153–162.
Idem. "Financial and Heraldic Records of the English Tournament." *J. Soc. Archivists* 2,5 (1962), 183–195.
Idem. *Spectacle, Pageantry, and the Early Tudor Policy*. Oxford: Clarendon, 1969.
D'Aquili, Eugene G., Charles D. Laughlin, and J. U. McManus. *The Spectrum of Ritual. A Biogenic Structural Analysis*. New York: Columbia UP, 1979.
Arens, William. "The Great American Football Ritual." *Natural History* 84(1975), 72–80.
Barlett, Vernon. *The Past of Pasttimes*. Edinburgh: Clark, 1969.
Beeler, John. *Warfare in England. 1066–1189*. Ithaca, N.Y.: Cornell UP, 1966.
Bintz, Julius. *Die volkthümlichen Leibesübungen des Mittelalters*. Hamburg: T. G. Meissner. (Reprint 2nd ed. 1880 Wiesbaden: M. Sändig, 1971.)
Birrell, Susan. "Sport as Ritual. Interpretations from Durkheim to Goffman." *Social Forces* 60,2 (1981), 354–376.
Bogeng, G. A. E. (ed.). *Geschichte des Sports aller Völker und Zeiten*. Leipzig: Semann, 1926.

Bouissac, Paul. *La mesure des gestes. Prolégomènes à la sémiotique gestuelle*. Den Haag: Mouton, 1973.

Brailsford, Dennis. *Sport and Society. From Elizabeth to Anne*. London: Routledge & Keegan Paul, 1969.

Brasch, Rudolph. *How Did Sport Begin? A Look into the Origins of Man at Play*. London: Longman, 1972.

Browne, R. B. *Rituals and Ceremonies in Popular Culture*. Bowling Green, Ohio: Bowling Green UP, 1980.

Bushnell, Amy. " 'The Demonic Game.' The Campaign to Stop Indian Pelota Playing in Spanish Florida. 1675–1684." *Americas* 35(July 1978), 1–19.

Carter, John Marshall. "A Note on Medieval Sports in Allen Guttmann's 'From Ritual to Record'." In idem, *Ludi Medi Aevi: Studies in the History of Medieval Sport*. Manhattan, Ks.: Military Affairs Publishing, 1981, 132–138.

Idem. "Sport, War, and the Three Orders of Feudal Society, 700–1300." In *Military Affairs* 49,3 (July 1985), 132–139.

Idem. "Sports and Recreation in Thirteenth Century England: The Evidence of the Eyre and Coroners' Rolls." In *Journal of Sport History* 15,2 (Summer 1988), 167–173.

Idem. *Sports and Pastimes of the Middle Ages*. Lanham; Md.: UP of America, 1988.

Ceard, Jean; Marie-Madelaine Fontaine and Jean-Claude Margolin (eds.). *Le corps à la renaissance*. Paris: CNRS, 1990.

Cheska, Alyce T. "Sports Spectacular: A Ritual Model of Power." *Int. Rev. Sp. Soc.* 14,2 (1979), 51–72.

Clare, Lucien. *La quintaine. La course de bague et le jeu des Tête*. Paris: CNRS, 1983.

Idem. "Le role de la noblesse dans les spectacles publics (1668)." In *Sports et civilisations*, vol. 5 edited by Louis Burgener et al. Bern: P. Lang, 1986, 68–75.

Clephan, Robert C. *The Tournament. Its Periods and Phases*. London: Methuen, 1918.

Contamine, Philippe. *Guerre, etat et société à fin du moyen age. Etudes sur les armée des rois de France. 1337–1494*. Paris: Mouton, 1972.

Cripps-Day, Francis H. *The History of the Tournament in England and in France*. London: B. Quaritch, 1918. (Reprint New York: AMS, 1982.)

Crowther, Nigel B. "Weightlifting in Antiquity: Achievement and Training." *Greek, Roman, and Byzantine Studies* 24(1977), 111–120.

Damm, Hans. "Vom Wesen sogenannter Leibesübungen bei Naturvölkern. Ein Beitrag zur Genese des Sports." *Studium Generale* 13,1 (1960). 1–10.

Decker, Wolfgang. *Sport und Spiel im Alten Ägypten*. München: C. H. Beck, 1987.

Deegan, Mary J., and Michael Stein. "American Drama and Ritual: Nebraska Football." *Int. Rev. Sp. Soc.* 13,3 1978), 31–44.

Denholm-Young, Noël. "The Tournament in the 13th Century," *Studies in Medieval History presented to F. M. Powicke* edited by Richard W. Hunt, W. A. Panten, et al. Oxford: Clarendon, 1948.

Desees, Julian. *Les Jeux sportifs de pelote-paume en Belgique du XIVe au XIXe siècles*. Brussels: Imp. du Centenaire, 1967.

Dillon, Viscount. "Tilting in Tudor Times." *Archeology J.* 55, 2nd ser., 5(1898), 296–321.

Idem. "Barriers and Foot Combats." *Archeology J.* 61, 2nd ser., 11 (1904), 275–308.

Diem, Carl. *Weltgeschichte des Sports*. Stuttgart: Cotta, 1960.

Dunleavy, Aidan O., and Andrew W. Miracle, Jr. "Sport: An Experimental Setting for the Development of a Theory of Ritual." In *Play as Context* edited by Alyce T. Cheska. West Point, N.Y.: Leisure, 1981, 118–126.

Duthie, J. H. . "Athletics: The Ritual of a Technological Society?" In *Play and Culture* edited by Helen B. Schwartzmann. West Point, N.Y.: Leisure, 1980, 91–98.

Eadem. "Sports Spectacular: The Social Ritual of Power." *Quest* (1978) no. 30, 58–71.

Eichberg, Henning. " 'Auf Zoll und Quintlein.' Sport und Quantifizierungsprozess in der frühen Neuzeit." *Archiv f. Kulturgesch.* 56(1974), 141–76.

Idem. "Zur kultur-historischen Relativität des Leistens in Sport und Spiel." *Sportwissenschaft* 6,1 (1976), 9–34.

Idem. "Recording and Quantifying Performance is not Natural—A Reply to Krüger and Ito." *Stadion* 3,2 (1977), 253–256.

Idem. *Leistung. Spannung. Geschwindigkeit. Sport und Tanz im gesellschaftlichen Wandel des 18./19. Jahrhunderts.* Stuttgart: Klett-Cotta, 1978.

Elias, Norbert, and Eric Dunning. *Quest for Excitement. Sport and Leisure in the Civilizing Process.* Oxford: Blackwell, 1986.

Fleckenstein, Josef. *Das ritterliche Turnier im Mittelalter.* Göttingen: Vandenhoeck & Ruprecht, 1985.

Foulkes, Charles. "Jousting Cheques of the 16th Century." *Archaeologica* 63 (1911/12), 31–50.

Francis, Philip Harwood. *A Study of Targets in Games.* London: Mitre, 1951.

Garcia y Bellido, Antonio. "El español C. Apuleius Diocles, el mas famoso corredor de carros de la antigüedad." *Citius-Altius-Fortius* 14 (1972), 5–17.

Gillmeister, Heiner. "Über Tennis und Tennispunkte. Ein Beitrag der Sprachwissenschaft zur Sportgeschichte." *Stadion* 3,2 (1977), 187–229.

Idem. *Aufschlag für Walther von der Vogelweide. Tennis seit dem Mittelalter.* München: Knaur, 1986.

Goffman, Erwing. *Interaction Ritual.* Garden City. N.J.: Doubleday, 1971.

Gori, Gigliola. *Gli etruschi e lo sport.* Urbino, 1986.

Gori, Pietro. *Il giuocco del clacio.* Firenze: Bemporad, 1898.

Grifi, Giampiero. *Ginnastica. Soria dell' educazione Fisica e dello sport.* Perugia: ISEF, 1985.

Guttmann, Allen. *From Ritual to Record. The Nature of Modern Sports.* New York: Columbia UP, 1978.

Idem. *Sport Spectators.* New York: Columbia UP, 1986.

Idem. *A Whole New Ballgame. An Interpretation of American Sports.* Chapel Hill, N.C.: North Carolina UP, 1988.

Hahn, Martin. *Die Leibesübungen im mittelalterlichen Volksleben.* Langensalza: Beyer, 1929. (Reprint Walluf: M. Sändig, 1972.)

Harris, Janet C. "Sport and Ritual. A Macroscopic Comparison of Form." In *The Paradoxes of Play* edited by John Loy. West Point, N.Y.: Leisure, 1982, 205–214.

Heywood, William. *Palio and Ponte. An Account of the Sports of Central Italy from the Age of Dante to the XXth Century.* London: Methuen, 1904. (Reprint New York: Hacker Art Books, 1969.)

Henderson, Robert W. "How Old Is the Game of Racquets?" *Bull. New York Public Library* 40 (May 1936), 5, 403–410.

Idem. *Ball, Bat and Bishop.* New York: Rockport, 1947.

Hopf, Wilhelm (ed.). *Die Veränderung des Sports ist gesellschaftlich. Diskussionsband.* Münster: Lit, 1986.

Hueppe, Ferdinand. "Kulturgeschichte der Leibesübungen im Mittelalter." In *Athletik* edited by Carl Krümmel. München: Lehmann, 1930, 28–51.

Huizinga, Johan. *Homo Ludens.* Boston: Beacon, 1955.

Huxley, John (ed.). "A Discussion on Ritualization of Behaviour in Animals and Man." *Philosophical Transactions of the Royal Society of London.* Ser. B. Biol. Sci. vol. 251. London: HMSP 1967, 211–526.

Jacquot, Jean (ed.). *Les Fêtes de la Renaissance.* Paris: CNRS, 1956, 1960, 1975 (3 vols).

Jusserand, Jean-Jules. *Les sports et jeux d'exercice dans l'ancienne France.* Paris: Plon-Nourrit. (Reprint Geneva: Slatkine, 1986 edited by Louis Burgener.)

Kilmer, Scott. "Sport as Ritual: A Theoretical Approach." *The Study of Play: Problems and Prospects* edited by David F. Lancy and B. Allan Tindall. West Point, N.Y.: Leisure, 1977, 44–49.

Klapp. Orrin E. *Ritual and Cult. A Sociological Interpretation.* Annals of American Sociology. Washington, D.C.: Public Affairs, 1956.

Kloeren, Maria. *Sport und Rekord. Kultursoziologische Untersuchungen zum England des 16. bis 18. Jahrhunderts.* Würzburg: Triltsch, 1935.

Kowald, Helmut. "Die Leibesübungen der Germanen bis zum Ende der deutschen Karolinger." Phil. Diss. Wien, 1934.

Kretzenbacher, Leopold. *Ringreiten, Rolandspiel, und Kufenstechen. Sportliches Reiterbrauchtum von heute als Erbe aus abendländischer Kulturgeschichte.* Klagenfurt: Gesch. Ver. Kärnten, 1966.

Krüger, Arnd, and John McClelland. eds. *Die Anfänge des modernen Sports in der Renaissance.* London: Arena, 1984.

Krüger, Gundolf. *Sportlicher Wettkampf auf Hawaii. Eine Konfiguration und ihr Wandel als Gegenstand ethnohistorischer Forschung.* Göttingen: Herodot, 1986.

Kyle, Donald G. *Athletics in Ancient Athens.* Leiden: E. J. Brill, 1987.

Lafond, Jean, and André Stegmann. *L'automme de la renaissance. 1580–1630.* Paris: Vrin, 1981.

Lensi, Alfredo. *Il giuoco del calcio fiorentino.* Firenze: Barfucci, 1931.

Luze, Albert de. *La magnifique histoire du jeu de paume.* Paris: Bossard, 1933.

Magoun, Francis P., Jr. "Football in Medieval England and in Middle English Literature." *Am. Hist. Rev.* 35, 1 (Oct. 1929), 33–45.

Mandell. Richard D. "The Invention of the Sports Record." *Stadion* 2 (1976), 250–264.

Idem. *Sport. A Cultural History.* New York: Columbia UP, 1984.

Manson, Michel. "La coule (soule) en Normandie au XVIième siècle d'après le Sire de Gouberville." In *Sports et civilisations,* vol. 4 edited by Louis Burgener et al. Bern: P. Lang, 1985, 97–106.

Marcelli, Marisa. *Educazione fisica e sport nel Rinascimento italiano.* Bologna: Patron, 1975.

Mason, Tony. *Sport in Britain.* London: Faber, 1988.

Masüger, Johann Baptist. *Schweizerbuch der alten Bewegungsspiele.* Zürich: Artemis, 1955.

McClelland, John. "L'Histoire des sports: Dimensions militaires et sémiotque." In *Sports et Cultures,* vol. 7 edited by Louis Burgener et al. Bern: P. Lang, 1986, 39–46.

Mehl, Jean-Michel. "Le jeu de paume: Un élément de la sociabilité aristocratique à la fin du moyen âge et au début de la renaissance." *Sport Histoire* 1,1 (1988), 19–30.

Meiners, Christoph. "Kurze Geschichte der Turniere." *Göttingesches Hist. Mag.* 4,4 (1817), 634–693.

Meyer, Werner. "Mittelalterliche Turniere." *Nachrichten des Schweizerischen Burgenvereins* 46(1973).

Miracle, Andrew W., Jr. "School Spirit as a Ritual By-Product: A View from Applied Anthropology." In *Play and Culture* edited by Helen B. Schwartzman. West Point, N.Y.: Leisure, 1980, 98–103.

Neuendorff, Edmund. *Geschichte der deutschen Leibesübung vom Beginn des 18. Jahrhundert bis zu Jahn. Mit einem Grundriβ der deutschen Leibesübung von den Urzeiten bis zum Beginn des 18. Jahrhunderts.* Dresden: Limpert, 1930.

Novak, Michael. "Games's the Thing. In Defence of Sports as Ritual." *Columbia Journalism Rev.* (May 15, 1976), 33–38.

Onians, R. . . . B. . . . The Origins of European Thought About the Body, the Mind, the Soul, the World, Time and Fate. Cambridge: Cambridge UP, 1954.

Orme, Nicholas. *Early British Swimming. 55BC–AD 1719.* Exeter: UP, 1983.

Poliakoff, Michael B. *Combat Sports in the Ancient World. Competition, Violence and Culture.* New Haven, Conn.: Yale UP, 1987.

Powell, George H. *Duelling Stories of the Sixteenth Century.* London: Bullen, 1904.

Reutler, Karl. "*Über die Leibesübungen der Primitiven. Ein Beitrag zur Ethnologie der Leibesübungen.*" Phil. Diss. Rostock, 1940.

Rosseau, E. L. "Great American Ritual: Watching Games." *Nation* 187,4 (1954), 188–191.

Rühl, Joachim K. *Die "Olympischen Spiele" Robert Dovers.* Heidelberg: C. Winter, 1975.

Sansone, David. *Greek Athletics and the Genesis of Sport.* Berkeley: University of California Press, 1988.

Saughneassy, J. D. *The Roots of Ritual.* Grand Rapids, Mich.: W. Eirdmans, 1973.

Schaufelberger, Walter. *Der Wettkampf in der alten Eidgenossenschaft. Von der Kulturgeschichte des Sports vom 13. bis 18. Jahrhundert.* Bern: P. Haupt, 1972.

Schröter, Harald. *Roger Ascham Toxophilus. The Schoole of Shootinge. London 1545.* St. Augustin: Richarz, 1983.

Strohmeyer, Hannes. "Grundzüge der adeligen Leibeserziehung in Österreich vom 13. bis zum 18. Jahrhundert." In *Beiträge zur Geschichte von Leibeserziehung und Sport in Österreich,* edited by idem. Wien: Wiss. Ges. Leibeserz. & Sport, 1980, 8–77.

Strutt, Joseph. *The Sports and Pastimes of the People of England.* London: Th. Tegg, 1834.

Turner, Victor W. *The Ritual Process. Structure and Anti-Structure.* Chicago: Aldine, 1969.

Ueberhorst, Horst (ed.). *Geschichte der Leibesübungen.* 6 vols. Berlin: Bartels & Wernitz, 1972–1989.

Ulmann, Jacques. *De la gymnastique aux sports modernes.* Paris: Vrin, 1971.

Vale, Juliet. *Edward III and Chivalry. Chivalric Society and Its Context 1270–1350.* Woodbridge: Boydell, 1982.

Vigarello, George. "Jeux 'sportifs' ancien, jeux de pari." *Sport Histoire* 1,1 (1988), 33–39.

Weiler, Ingomar. *Der Sport bei den Völkern der Alten Welt*. Darmstadt: Wissenschaftliche, 1981.

Wymer, Norman. *Sport in England. A History of Two Thousand Years of Games and Pasttimes*. London: Harrap, 1949.

Young, Alan. *Tudor and Jacobean Tournaments*. New York: Sheridan House, 1987.

Index

About the Editors and Contributors

JOHN MARSHALL CARTER teaches at Oglethorpe University in Atlanta.

WOLFGANG DECKER is a professor in the Institut für Sportgeschichte at the Sport University of Cologne.

HENNING EICHBERG is a professor at Idraetsforsk, Gerlev Idraetshøjskole, Slagelse, Denmark.

ALLEN GUTTMANN is professor of American Studies at Amherst College.

AKIRA ITO is a professor of sport history, Sophia University, Tokyo, Japan.

OVE KORSGAARD is a professor at Idraetsforsk, Gerlev Idraetshøjskole, Slagelse, Denmark.

ARND KRÜGER is a professor at the Institut für Sportwissenschaften at the University of Göttingen.

GUNDOLF KRÜGER is head of educational services of the anthropological museum of Baden-Württemberg at Stuttgart.

JOHN McCLELLAND teaches in the French Department at Victoria College, University of Toronto.

DONALD PARKERSON teaches quantitative methods and their use in history at East Carolina University.

DIETRICH RAMBA teaches at the Institut für Sportwissenschaften at the University of Göttingen.

JOACHIM RÜHL teaches at the Institut für Sport Leichtathletik und Turnen at the Sport University of Cologne.